TELL ME WHAT?

CHANCELLOR PRESS

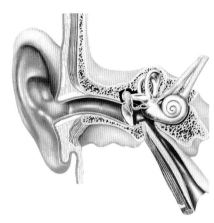

First published in 2002 by Chancellor Press,
an imprint of Bounty Books, a division of
Octopus Publishing Group Ltd
Reprinted 2004, 2005, 2007

Revised edition published in 2010 by Chancellor Press

This edition published in 2014 by Chancellor Press,
an imprint of Bounty Books, a division of
Octopus Publishing Group Ltd
Carmelite House
50 Victoria Embankment
London, EC4Y 0DZ
www.octopusbooks.co.uk

An Hachette UK Company
www.hachette.co.uk

Reprinted 2016

ISBN: 978-0-753728-05-5

Printed in China

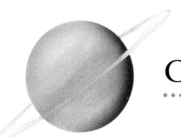

CONTENTS

. . . .

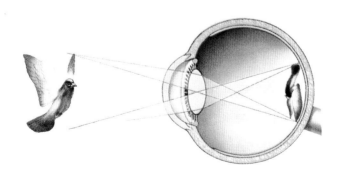

OUR

WORLD

CONTENTS

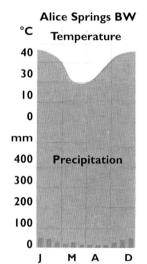

Alice Springs BW

°C **Temperature**

40
30
10
0

mm

400 **Precipitation**
300
200
100
0

J   M   A   D

WHAT DEFINES A DAY?

For early peoples, the only changes that were truly regular, were the motions of objects in the sky. The most obvious of these changes was the alternate daylight and darkness, caused by the rising and setting of the sun. Each of these cycles of the sun came to be called a day. Another regular change in the sky was the change in the visible shape of the moon. Each cycle of the moon's changing shape takes about 29½ days, or a month. The cycle of the seasons gave people an even longer unit of time.

There is no regular change in the sky that lasts seven days, to represent the week. The seven-day week came from the Jewish custom of observing a Sabbath (day of rest) every seventh day. The division of a day into 24 hours, an hour into 60 minutes, and a minute into 60 seconds probably came from the ancient Babylonians.

FACT FILE

Some clock faces are divided into 24 hours. On such a clock, 9 a.m. would be shown as 0900 and 4 p.m. would be 1600. This system avoids confusion between the morning and evening hours.

21 JUNE

North Pole: 24 hours daylight

N

13.5 hours daylight

SUN'S RAYS

12 hours daylight

0°

10.5 hours daylight

S

South Pole: 24 hours darkness

WHAT IS A HEMISPHERE?

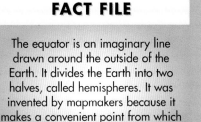

FACT FILE

The equator is an imaginary line drawn around the outside of the Earth. It divides the Earth into two halves, called hemispheres. It was invented by mapmakers because it makes a convenient point from which to measure distances.

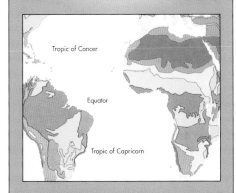

Tropic of Cancer

Equator

Tropic of Capricorn

Hemisphere is the name given to any half of the globe. It comes from a Greek word that means half a sphere.

Geographers divide the Earth into hemispheres by using the equator as a boundary line. All areas north of the equator make up the Northern Hemisphere. All areas to the south make up the Southern Hemisphere.

The earth may also be divided into a land hemisphere and a water hemisphere. The land hemisphere includes the half of the earth with the most land. Its middle lies near London, England. The other half of the earth, mostly water, makes up the water hemisphere. Its middle lies near New Zealand.

North Pole: 24 hours darkness

21 DECEMBER

10.5 hours daylight

12 hours daylight 0°

13.5 hours daylight

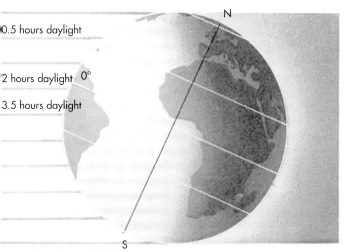

N

S

South Pole: 24 hours daylight

WHAT IS A TIME ZONE?

If every community used a different time, travellers would be confused and many other problems would be created. To avoid all such problems, standard time zones were established. These zones were set up so there would be a difference of one hour between a place on the eastern edge of a time zone and a place on the western edge if each were on its own local time. But under the time zone system, each of these places is not on its own local time. The local time at the meridian (line) of longitude that runs through the middle of the zone is used by all places within the zone. Thus, time throughout the zone is the same.

12 midnight   2AM   4AM   6AM   8AM   10AM   12

Reykjavik
Copenh
Greenwich (London)
Pa
Lisbon

Sunday

International date line

Vancouver
San Francisco
Los Angeles
Honolulu
Toronto
Chicago
New York
Miami
Mexico City
Caracas
Rio de Janeiro
Buenos Aires

TIME ZONES

Zones using GMT (Greenwich Mean Time)

Half-hour zones

Zones slow of GMT

Zones fast of GMT

The time when it is 12 noon at Greenwich

FACT FILE

The United States and Canada each have six standard time zones. Each zone uses a time one hour different from its adjacent zones.

WHAT IS THE GREENWICH MERIDIAN?

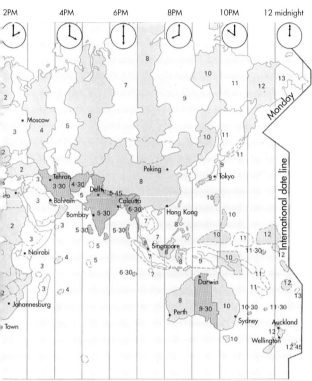

2PM 4PM 6PM 8PM 10PM 12 midnight

Meridians are imaginary north-south lines that pass from the North to the South Pole. The Greenwich meridian passes through the site of the Royal Observatory at Greenwich in south-east London. It is known as the prime meridian and positions east or west of it are measured in relation to it: New York is 74°W and Sydney 151°10'E. The Greenwich meridian is also the base for the time zones. In zones east of Greenwich, the clocks are ahead, so at midnight in London it is 3a.m. in Moscow. In zones west of Greenwich, the clocks are behind, so at midnight in London, in San Francisco it is 4p.m. The International Date Line is where the days change, so when it is Sunday just east of it, it is Monday to the west of it.

FACT FILE

In the mid-1950's, the Royal Greenwich Observatory was moved from Greenwich to Herstmonceux Castle in East Sussex to avoid interference from London lights and interference from electric train lines.

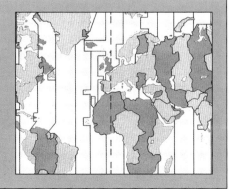

WHAT IS THE DEPTH OF THE PACIFIC OCEAN?

The Pacific Ocean, the largest and deepest of the world's four oceans, covers more than a third of the Earth's surface and contains more than half of its free water. The floor of the Pacific Ocean, which has an average depth of around 14,000 feet (4,300 m), is largely a deep-sea plain. The name Pacific, which means *peaceful*, was given to it by the Portuguese navigator Ferdinand Magellan in 1520. The Pacific is the oldest of the existing ocean basins, its oldest rocks having been dated at 200 million years.

The Pacific Ocean is bounded on the east by the North and South American continents; on the north by the Bering Strait; on the west by Asia, the Malay Archipelago, and Australia; and on the south by Antarctica.

360 million sq km of Earth's surface is covered by water

FACT FILE

The Pacific Ocean contains more than 30,000 islands; their total land area, however, amounts to only one-quarter of one percent of the ocean's surface area.

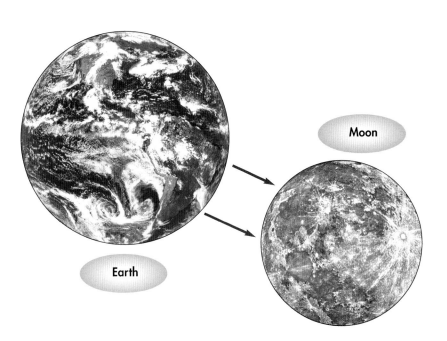

Moon

Earth

WHAT CAUSES TIDES?

Tides are the periodic rise and fall of all ocean waters, caused by the gravitational pull of the Moon. The Moon's pull on the Earth draws the ocean water towards the Moon, making the water form a huge swell. This is known as a high tide. Water closest to the Moon will always be the point of the highest tide. As the Earth spins around, different oceans become the closest stretch of water to the Moon. This is why all oceans and seas have different points of high tide at different times of the day or night.

FACT FILE

Spring tides are tides with unusually high ranges twice per month when the Sun, Earth, and Moon are in line. They can be especially high in the spring and autumn.

WHAT ARE OCEAN TRENCHES?

Trenches are the deepest parts of the ocean. Many trenches occur in the Pacific Ocean, especially in its western portion. Most trenches are long, narrow and deep, 3-4 km (2-2.5 mi) below the surrounding sea floor. The greatest depth anywhere in the ocean is found in the Mariana Trench southeast of Japan. It plunges more than 11 km (6.8 mi) below sea level. Frequent earthquakes and volcanic eruptions occur along the trenches.

FACT FILE

For centuries, most people assumed that the cold, black depths of the ocean supported little or no life. Scientists have since discovered a great variety of living things in the deep sea.

Deep-sea fish are very different from those found in shallow waters

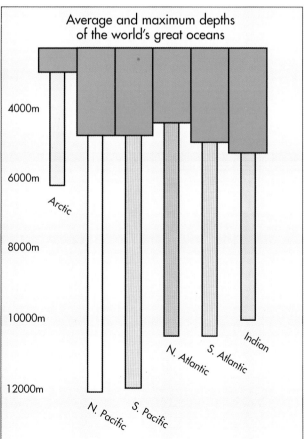

Average and maximum depths of the world's great oceans

4000m

6000m

Arctic

8000m

10000m

N. Atlantic

S. Atlantic

Indian

12000m

N. Pacific

S. Pacific

WHAT ARE CURRENTS?

The ocean waters are moved by the wind on their surface and by movements within the ocean. These currents are able to transfer a great amount of heat around the Earth as they move and thus play a part in climate control. The spinning of the Earth dictates the way the water circulates. In the northern hemisphere it moves clockwise and in the southern hemisphere, anti-clockwise. Ocean currents vary in the summer and winter and a change in wind direction can change the current, influencing the weather in a particular country. A cold ocean current makes the weather colder and a warm one, warmer.

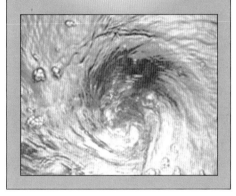

FACT FILE

A whirlpool is a mass of water which spins around and around rapidly and with great force. It may occur when opposing currents meet, or it may be caused by the action of the wind.

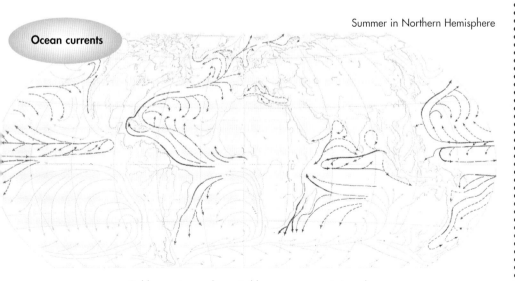

Summer in Northern Hemisphere

Ocean currents

Cold currents are shown in blue, warm currents in red

200 million years ago

135 million years ago

Present day

150 million years' time

WHAT DID THE CONTINENTS LOOK LIKE BEFORE?

When the Earth formed, the lighter elements floated to the surface, where they cooled to form a crust. The first rocks were formed over 3,500 years ago, but they have not remained static. The coastlines on either side of the Atlantic appear to fit together like a jigsaw, and it is thought that all the land masses were once joined together, forming a super continent called Pangaea. Changed by forces outside and within the earth, Pangaea divided to form the continents we know today.

FACT FILE

Movement of the land is still taking place as India and Asia are colliding, forming the Himalayas. This movement is called continental drift.

WHAT ARE PLATE TECTONICS?

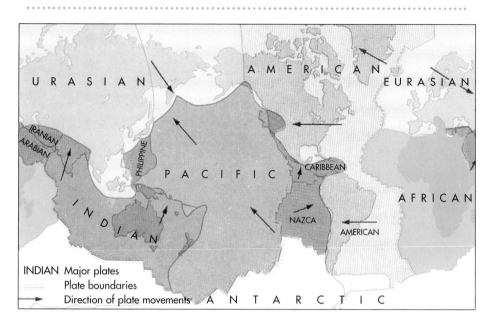

U R A S I A N
A M E R I C A N
EURASIAN
IRANIAN
ARABIAN
PHILIPPINE
P A C I F I C
CARIBBEAN
AFRICAN
NAZCA
AMERICAN
I N D I A N

INDIAN Major plates
         Plate boundaries
         Direction of plate movements A N T A R C T I C

Plate tectonics is a scientific theory by which the origin of most of the major features seen on the Earth's surface are explained. This theory tells us that the Earth has an outer shell made up of about 30 rigid pieces, called tectonic plates, some of which are vast: most of the Pacific ocean covers a single plate. The movement of the plates is responsible for the faulting and folding of the earth's crust, creating volcanoes, mountain ranges and so on. The plates are able to move on a layer of molten rock beneath, which is so hot that it flows though it remains solid. The plates move up to 10 cm (4 ins) a year.

FACT FILE

Plates have been moving about for hundreds of millions of years. So, in spite of their very low speeds, some of them have moved vast distances over the past several hundred million years.

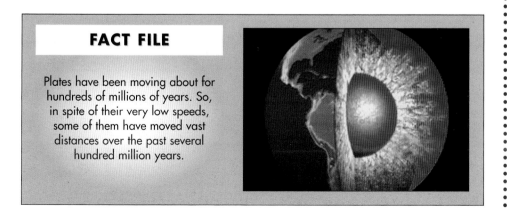

WHAT SHAPES THE SEA-FLOOR?

The bottom of the ocean has features as varied as those on land. Huge plains spread out across the ocean floor, and long mountain chains rise toward the surface. Volcanoes erupt from the ocean bottom, and deep valleys cut through the floor. In the early 1960s, a theory called *sea-floor spreading* provided some explanation. According to the theory, the sea floor itself moves, carrying the continents along. Circulating movements deep within the earth's mantle make the sea floor move. The circulating movements carry melted rock up to the mid-ocean ridges and force it into the central valleys of the ridges. As the melted rock cools and hardens, it forms new sea floor and pushes the old floor and the continents away from the ridges.

FACT FILE

A hot vent is a chimney-like structure on the ocean floor that discharges hot, mineral-rich water. Scientists first observed hot vents in 1977, in the Galapagos Rift, a region on the floor of the Pacific Ocean.

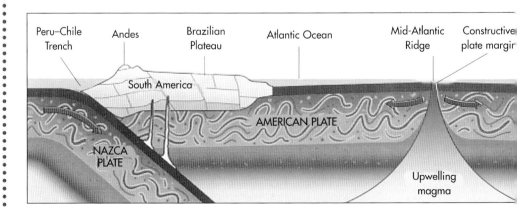

Peru–Chile Trench · Andes · Brazilian Plateau · Atlantic Ocean · Mid-Atlantic Ridge · Constructive plate margin · South America · AMERICAN PLATE · NAZCA PLATE · Upwelling magma

WHAT ARE CONTINENTAL SHELVES?

FACT FILE

The continental rise consists of sediment from the continental shelf that accumulates at the bottom of the slope. These deposits can extend up to about 1,000 km (600 miles) from the slope.

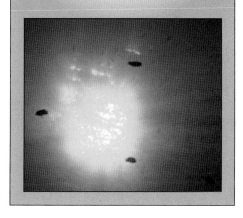

The continental margin forms the part of the seabed that borders the continents. It consists of (1) the continental shelf, (2) the continental slope, and (3) the continental rise.

The continental shelf is the submerged land at the edge of the continents. It begins at the shoreline and gently slopes underwater to an average depth of about 130 m (430 ft). The width of the continental shelf averages 75 km (47 miles). In certain areas, such as parts of the Arctic region, the shelf extends as far as 1,600 km (1,000 miles). In some other areas, particularly those bordering much of the Pacific, it measures only 1.6 km (1 mile) or less. Valleys of varying depths cut through the shelf.

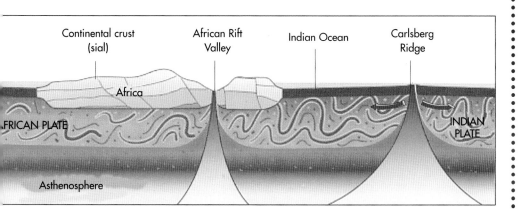

Continental crust (sial)   African Rift Valley   Indian Ocean   Carlsberg Ridge

Africa

AFRICAN PLATE   INDIAN PLATE

Asthenosphere

WHAT CAUSES LAND EROSION?

Erosion is a natural process by which rock and soil are broken loose from the earth's surface at one location and moved to another. Erosion changes land by wearing down mountains, filling in valleys, and making rivers appear and disappear. It is usually a slow and gradual process that occurs over thousands, even millions of years.

Erosion begins with a process called weathering. In this process, environmental factors break rock and soil into smaller pieces and loosen them from the earth's surface. A chief cause is the formation of ice. As water freezes, it expands with great force. As a result, when it freezes inside the crack of a rock, it can break the rock apart.

FACT FILE

Erosion can be speeded up by such human activities as farming and mining. One of the most harmful effects of erosion is that it robs farmland of productive topsoil.

Desert erosion

③

④

① ②

WHAT ERODES THE DESERTS?

A desert landscape includes various kinds of surface features created by water and wind erosion and by deposits of silt, sand, and other sediments. The drainage system is made up of normally dry streams called *arroyos*. After a rainfall, water fills the stream channels called *wadi* ①. The rapidly flowing water cuts away the rocks of desert mountains and carries sediments to the mouth of mountain canyons. There, deposits of sediments create fan-shaped forms known as alluvial fans ②. Sometimes, the streams carry water into low areas in the desert plains and form temporary lakes. The water that collects in these lakes either evaporates or seeps into the ground. Water erosion also creates big flat-topped hills known as *mesas* ③ and smaller flat-topped hills called *buttes* ④.

FACT FILE

Vast regions covered by sand and dunes are called sand seas. Sand seas cover large areas in desert regions of Africa, Asia, and Australia.

19

WHAT IS A GLACIER?

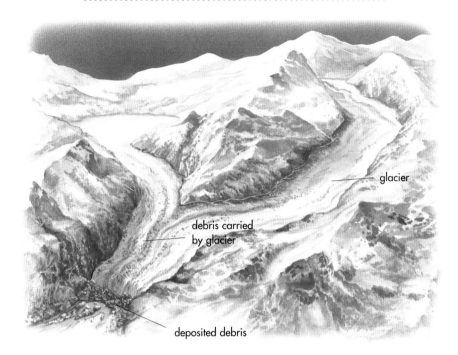

glacier

debris carried by glacier

deposited debris

Glaciers begin to form when more snow falls during the winter than melts and evaporates in summer. The excess snow gradually builds up in layers. Its increasing weight causes the snow crystals under the surface to become compact, grain-like pellets called firn. At depths of 15 m (50 ft) or more, the firn is further compressed into dense crystals of glacial ice. The ice eventually becomes so thick that it moves under the pressure of its own great weight.

FACT FILE

Glaciers have shaped most of the world's highest mountains, carving out huge valleys. The lakes are formed from flooded glacial valleys that become dammed by debris as the glacier melts.

WHAT IS AN ICE SHEET?

Over 10,000 years ago about a third of the land surface was covered by ice. Today a tenth is still covered in ice. Ice sheets can cover very large areas and can be very thick. The world's largest ice sheet covers most of Antarctica and is very slow moving.

Antarctica covers about 14,000,000 square km (5,400,000 square miles). It is larger in area than either Europe or Australia. However, Antarctica would be the smallest continent if it did not have its icecap. This icy layer, which averages approximately 2,200 m (7,100 ft) thick, increases Antarctica's surface area and also makes Antarctica the highest continent in terms of average elevation.

FACT FILE

There is a huge area of ice in the Arctic, but this is quite thin and floats on the ocean. Today, many scientists think global warming is causing the ice to melt and sea level to rise, increasing the threat of floods.

WHAT SHAPES A RIVER?

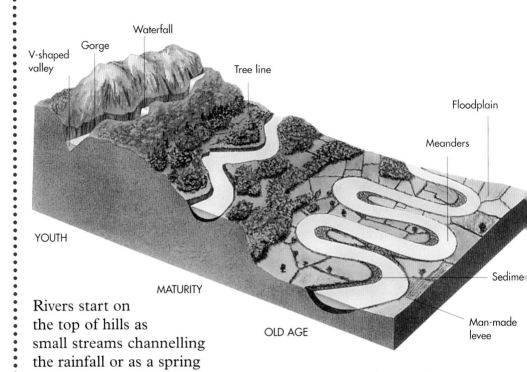

V-shaped valley

Gorge

Waterfall

Tree line

Floodplain

Meanders

YOUTH

MATURITY

OLD AGE

Sedime

Man-made levee

Rivers start on the top of hills as small streams channelling the rainfall or as a spring releasing ground water. They begin to cut at and change the landscape on the way to the sea. In the highlands the water can move very quickly and has a lot of power. The river can cut deep gorges and V-shaped valleys in the softer rocks. In the harder rocks they can form waterfalls. The river moves rocks and pebbles along its bed by bouncing and rolling. The lighter sediments are carried or dissolved in the water. When they reach the more gentle slopes the river becomes wider and moves more slowly. Mud and sand is dropped when the river floods and forms ridges along the river bank. When the river reaches the lower plains it begins to meander.

FACT FILE

The further a river is from its source on a mountainside, the slower the water travels. This is because the river eventually reaches flatter ground and widens before it reaches the sea.

WHAT SHAPES THE COASTS?

FACT FILE

Many cliffs on the coast are made up of chalk. Chalk is formed from the skeletons of millions and millions of tiny animals called foraminifera. It is a sedimentary rock that formed millions of years ago beneath shallow seas.

Coastlines are constantly changing: they are either being eroded or built up. The waves are very powerful and can remove a large amount of material from a coastline, especially during a storm. The sand and pebbles removed from the coastline are carried by the sea and can be dropped further along a coast or out at sea.

Many coastal features can be made by the steady erosion of the cliffs and headlands such as sand dunes, spits and salt marshes. A beach can make the waves less powerful and reduce the amount of erosion of the coast. Steep cliffs and wave-cut platforms can be formed in areas of hard rock. A bay can be carved out in an area where hard rock has soft rock between it.

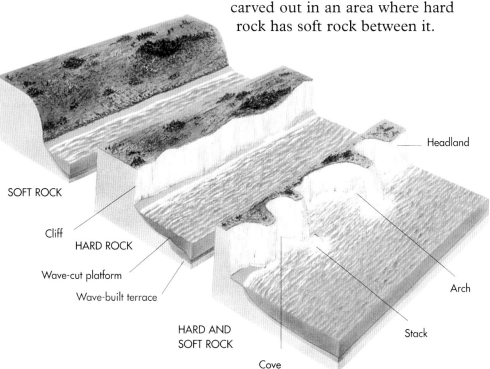

SOFT ROCK

Cliff

HARD ROCK

Wave-cut platform

Wave-built terrace

HARD AND
SOFT ROCK

Cove

Headland

Arch

Stack

WHAT IS CLIMATE?

FACT FILE

Mountains, such as the Rockies in North America, have a typical alpine climate because of their height.

Climatic zones

Af	Am	Aw	BS	BW	Cw	
Tropical climates			Dry climates		Warm temperate clima	

Climate is the word we use to describe the seasonal pattern of hot and cold, wet and dry weather, averaged over 30 years. There are four types of climate: these are tropical, (hot and wet) desert (dry), temperate, (mild) and polar (cold). As different parts of the earth are closer to the sun for longer, the climate varies in different countries. Those nearest the equator are the hottest. Those nearest the poles are the coldest. Winds and ocean currents distribute the heat around the earth. The weather pattern in different regions will also be altered by the changing seasons and some areas routinely have a higher level of annual rainfall than others, whilst some countries remain very dry.

WHAT IS A SAVANNA?

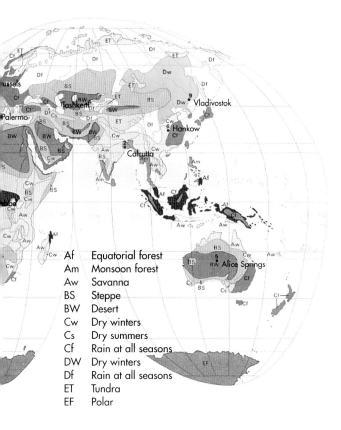

Af Equatorial forest
Am Monsoon forest
Aw Savanna
BS Steppe
BW Desert
Cw Dry winters
Cs Dry summers
Cf Rain at all seasons
DW Dry winters
Df Rain at all seasons
ET Tundra
EF Polar

Cf	Dw	Df	ET	EF
	Cool temperate climates		Cold climates	

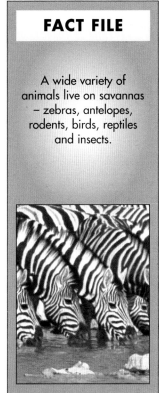

A Savanna, also spelled savannah, is a grassland with widely scattered trees and shrubs. Most savannas are in the tropics and lie between deserts and rain forests. Savannas cover more than two-fifths of Africa and large areas of Australia, India, and South America. They occur in regions that have both rainy and dry seasons. The growth of trees on savannas is limited by the dry season, which may last up to five months. When the dry season begins, grasses stop growing and turn brown, and most trees shed their leaves. Only the most drought-resistant trees can survive. Most savanna grasses grow in clumps. Acacias, baobabs, and palms are some common savanna trees.

WHAT IS PRECIPITATION?

Rain falls throughout most of the world. In the tropics, almost all precipitation is rain. Rain is precipitation that consists of drops of water. Raindrops form in clouds when microscopic droplets of water grow or when particles of ice melt before reaching the ground. In inland areas of Antarctica, all precipitation falls as snow.

Rain does not fall evenly over the earth. Some regions are always too dry, and others too wet. A region that usually gets enough rain may suddenly have a serious dry spell, and another region may be flooded with too much rain.

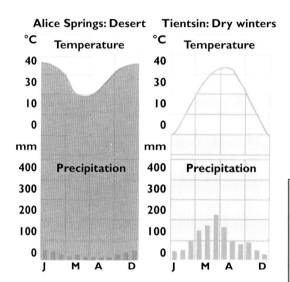

Alice Springs: Desert

°C Temperature

40
30
10
0

mm Precipitation

400
300
200
100
0

J M A D

Tientsin: Dry winters

°C Temperature

40
30
10
0

mm Precipitation

400
300
200
100
0

J M A D

Entebbe: Equatorial forest

°C Temperature

40
30
10
0

mm Precipitation

400
300
200
100
0

J M A D

Hyderabad: Monsoon forest

°C Temperature

40
30
10
0

mm Precipitation

400
300
200
100
0

J M A D

FACT FILE

The islands of the Seychelles are very humid and have high levels of rainfall which feeds the tropical rainforests. The average annual rainfall ranges from 132 cm (52 in) on some of the coral islands to 234 cm (92 in) on Mahé.

What causes flooding?

Flooding occurs when water cannot drain away fast enough in the rivers. In areas of non-porous rocks, water runs off the land very quickly and streams and rivers soon overflow. Flooding also happens when winter snows thaw in spring. Huge floods cover parts of Siberia every spring, when snow melts while the rivers are still iced up. Low-lying coastal lands are vulnerable to flooding, especially when gales and high tides cause water to flow inland. Low-lying Bangladesh is particularly liable to this kind of flooding. In addition, melting snow in the Himalayan mountains adds huge amounts of water to Bangladesh's rivers, increasing the flood risk.

FACT FILE

Many of the world's cities are low lying and threatened by flooding. Bangkok, in Thailand, and Venice, in Italy, are typical old cities built near water because they relied on shipping.

WHAT ARE THE MOST EXTREME TEMPERATURES RECORDED?

FACT FILE

Over millions of years the human body has altered to suit the climate of the regions we inhabit. In general the hotter the region, the darker the skin of its inhabitants.

Libya and the Antarctic have recorded the most extreme temperatures. The hottest shade temperature was in Libya in 1922, when the temperature in the Sahara desert reached 58°C. Temperatures nearly as high as this were recorded in Death Valley in the USA in 1913. The coldest ever recorded temperature was in Antarctica in 1983, when Russian scientists measured a temperature low of –89.2°C. The longest heatwave recorded was in Marble Bar, Australia when the temperature stayed above 38°C. It lasted for 162 days from 23 October 1923 to 7 April 1924.

30°C
20°C
10°C
0°C
–10°C
–20°C
–30°C
–40°C

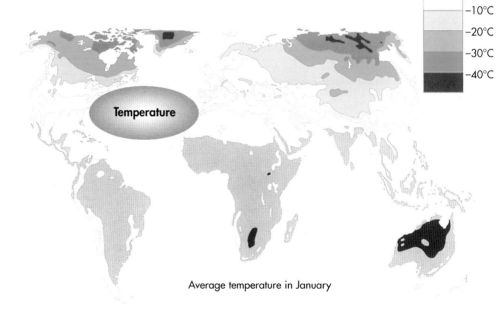

Temperature

Average temperature in January

WHAT IS A DROUGHT?

Drought is a condition that results when the average rainfall for an area drops far below the normal amount for a long period of time. In areas that are not irrigated, the lack of rain causes farm crops to wither and die. Higher than normal temperatures usually accompany periods of drought. These high temperatures increase the stresses on plants and add to the crop damage. Forest and grass fires are more frequent and spread quickly due to the dry conditions. Much valuable timberland and rangeland has been burned during major droughts. Poor management of the soil can frequently lead to wind erosion. Often the dry and crumbled topsoil is blown away by hot, dry winds. Streams, ponds, and wells regularly dry up during a drought, and animals suffer and may even die because of the lack of water.

3,000mm
2,000mm
1,000mm
500mm
250mm

Rainfall

Average annual precipitation

TELL ME WHAT : OUR WORLD

WHAT IS SALINE WATER?

Most of the water on Earth is saline (containing salt) and is found in the oceans. The ocean provides us with many things. It is far more than a place for swimming, boating, and other recreation. The oceans serve as a source of food, energy, and minerals. Ships use the oceans to carry cargo between continents. But above all else, the sea helps keep the earth's climate healthy by regulating the air temperature and by supplying the moisture for rainfall. If there were no oceans, life could not exist on our planet. Every natural element can be found in the waters of the oceans. But the oceans are especially known for their salts. Seawater contains, on average, about 3½ percent salts. Six elements account for 99 percent of an ocean's salinity (saltiness). They are, in order of amount, chloride, sodium, sulphur (as sulphate), magnesium, calcium, and potassium. Most of the salty material in the sea consists of the compound sodium chloride, or ordinary table salt.

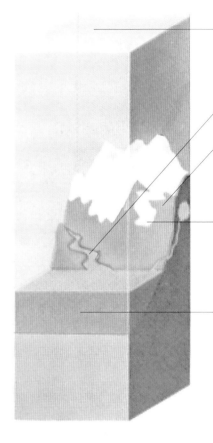

FACT FILE

Many salts in the ocean come chiefly from the wearing away of rocks on land. As rocks break down, rivers carry the salts and other material the rocks consist of to the ocean. Material released by volcanoes and undersea springs also contributes salts to the ocean.

WHAT IS IRRIGATION?

Irrigation is the watering of land by artificial methods. It provides water for plant growth in areas that have long periods of little or no rainfall. The water used for irrigation is taken from lakes, rivers, streams, and wells.

Irrigation is used chiefly in three types of climates. In desert regions, such as Egypt and the Southwestern United States, farming would be impossible without irrigation. In regions with seasonal rainfall, such as California and Italy, irrigation makes farming possible even during dry months.

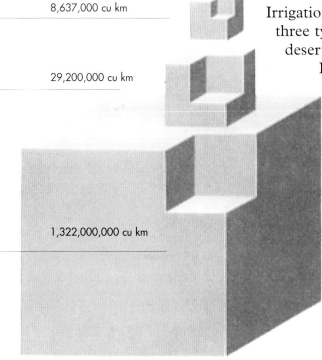

13,000 cu km

230,250 cu km

8,637,000 cu km

29,200,000 cu km

1,322,000,000 cu km

FACT FILE

In the mid-1980's, about 550 million acres (220 million hectares) of land were under irrigation throughout the world. Rice is one of the world's most important food crops. Lowland rice is grown in flat fields that are flooded by irrigation.

WHAT IS THE WATER CYCLE?

Hydrology is the study of the movement and distribution of the waters of the Earth. People use billions of gallons of fresh water every day. In nature, water circulates through a system called the *water cycle* or *hydrologic cycle*. This cycle begins when heat from the sun causes ocean water to evaporate. The vaporized water in the atmosphere gradually cools and forms clouds. The water eventually falls as rain or snow. Most rain and snow falls back into the oceans. But some falls on the land and flows back to the seas, completing the cycle.

FACT FILE

There are two main sources of fresh water: (1) surface water and (2) ground water. Surface water flows over the land in lakes, rivers, and streams. Ground water seeps through the soil or through tiny cracks in rock.

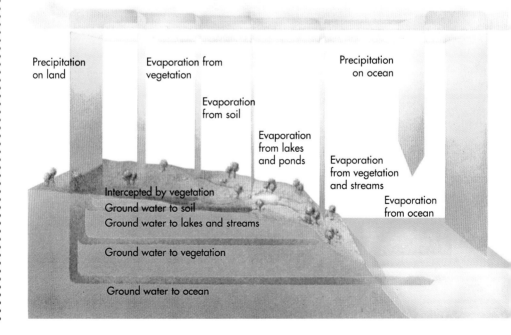

Precipitation on land

Evaporation from vegetation

Precipitation on ocean

Evaporation from soil

Evaporation from lakes and ponds

Evaporation from vegetation and streams

Intercepted by vegetation
Ground water to soil
Ground water to lakes and streams

Evaporation from ocean

Ground water to vegetation

Ground water to ocean

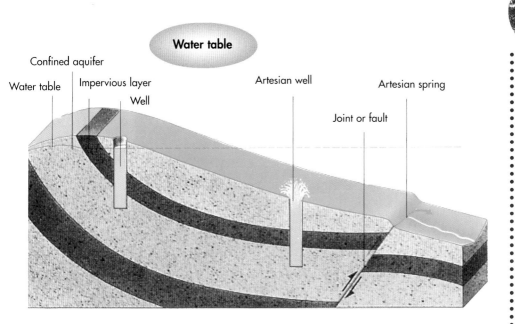

Water table

Confined aquifer

Water table   Impervious layer   Artesian well   Artesian spring

Well   Joint or fault

WHAT IS THE WATER TABLE?

Ground water is water beneath the surface of the earth. It is the source of water for wells and many springs. Ground water accumulates chiefly from rain and melted snow that filters through the soil. It also collects from water that seeps into the ground from lakes and ponds. The water settles into the pores and cracks of underground rocks and into the spaces between grains of sand and pieces of gravel. A layer or bed of such porous material that yields useful amounts of ground water is called an aquifer. Wells are drilled down to aquifers to draw ground water to the surface.

The level of ground water, called the *water table*, drops when more water is withdrawn than can be replaced naturally. Many regions of the world are using up the ground water faster than aquifers are being replenished.

FACT FILE

Pollution of ground water is a serious problem, especially near cities and industrial sites. Pollutants that seep into the ground result from contaminated surface water, leaks from sewer pipes and septic tanks, and chemical spills.

WHAT IS A TSUNAMI?

Earthquakes on the ocean floor can give a tremendous push to surrounding seawater and create one or more large, destructive waves called tsunamis; also known as seismic sea waves. Tsunamis may build to heights of more than 30 m (100 ft) when they reach shallow water near shore. In the open ocean, tsunamis typically move at speeds of 800 to 970 km (500 to 600 miles) per hour. They can travel great distances while diminishing little in size and can flood coastal areas thousands of miles from their source.

In 2004, the Indian Ocean Tsunami killed hundreds of thousands of people and destroyed the coastline.

Another form of tsunami is called a storm surge. This is caused when a violent storm whips up huge waves. In 1970 a storm surge and cyclone hit Bangladesh, killing 266,000 people. A further 10,000 people were killed when another one struck in 1985.

FACT FILE

Probably the best-known gauge of earthquake intensity is the local Richter magnitude scale, developed in 1935 by United States seismologist Charles F. Richter.

WHAT IS AN EYEWALL?

A storm achieves hurricane status when its winds exceed 118 km (74 miles) per hour. By the time a storm reaches hurricane intensity, it usually has a well-developed eye at its middle. Surface pressure drops to its lowest in the eye. In the eyewall (or the eye of the storm), warm air spirals upwards, creating the hurricane's strongest winds. The speed of the winds in the eyewall is related to the diameter of the eye. Just as ice skaters spin faster when they pull their arms in, a hurricane's winds blow faster if its eye is small. If the eye widens, the winds decrease.

Heavy rains fall from the eyewall and from bands of dense clouds that swirl around the eyewall. These bands, called rainbands, can produce more than 5 cm (2 ins) of rain per hour. The hurricane draws large amounts of heat and moisture from the sea.

WHAT IS ACID RAIN?

FACT FILE

Adding lime to lakes and rivers and their drainage areas temporarily neutralizes their acidity. But the neutralization may have harmful side effects.

Acid rain is a term for rain, snow, sleet, or other wet precipitation that is polluted by such acids as sulphuric acid and nitric acid. Acid rain harms thousands of lakes, rivers, and streams worldwide, killing fish and other wildlife. It also damages buildings, bridges, and statues. High concentrations of acid rain can harm forests and soil.

Acid rain forms when vaporized water in the air reacts with certain chemical compounds. These compounds, including sulphur dioxide and nitrogen oxides, come largely from the burning of coal, gasoline, and oil. Most vehicles, factories, and power plants burn such fuels for energy.

Regions affected by acid rain include large parts of eastern North America, Scandinavia and central Europe, and parts of Asia. Since about the 1950s, the problem has increased in rural areas. This has occurred because the use of taller smokestacks in urban areas has enabled the winds to transport pollutants farther from their sources.

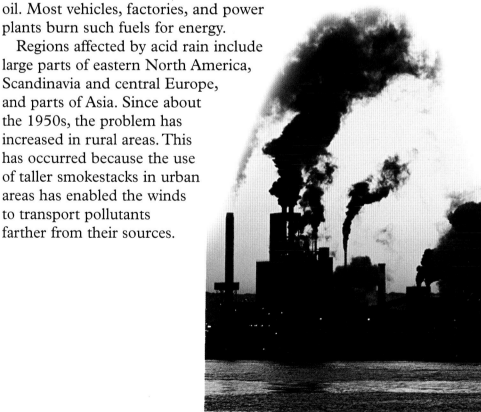

WHAT IS DEFORESTATION?

People are rapidly destroying the world's rain forests. In 1950, rain forests covered about 22,533,000 square km (8,700,000 sq miles) of the earth. This area would cover about three-quarters of Africa. Today, less than half the original extent of the earth's rain forest remains. In such regions as Madagascar, Sumatra, and the Atlantic coast of Brazil, only small patches still stand. Few rain forest species can adjust to severe disturbance of their habitat. Most perish when people clear large areas of forest. Scientists estimate that tropical deforestation wipes out about 7,500 species per year. Commercial logging, agriculture, mining and hydroelectric dams have all damaged or wiped out extensive areas of rain forest.

FACT FILE

Rain forests benefit people in four major ways. They provide (1) economic, (2) scientific, (3) environmental, and (4) recreational value.

THE

HUMAN BODY

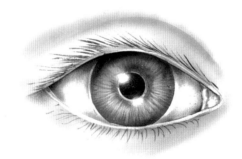

CONTENTS

• • • • • • • • • • • • • • • • • • •

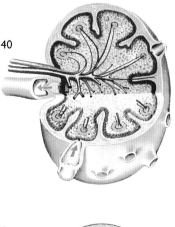

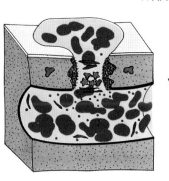

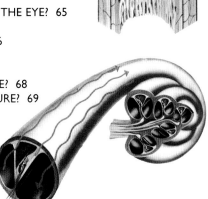

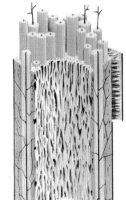

WHAT ARE THE MAIN ORGANS OF THE BODY?

Human anatomy is generally studied by looking at the many and varied organs of the body. Most of these can be grouped together into different systems on the basis of these organs and their accompanying structures that work together to perform specific body functions. The groups are as follows: Skeletal, Muscular, Nervous, Endocrine, Respiratory, Cardio-vascular, Lymph-vascular, Digestive, Excretory and Reproductive. The largest organ in the body is in fact the skin. In an adult it covers about 2km² and not only envelops the whole body in a protective waterproof layer, but is also part of the heat-regulating system. The liver is the most complicated organ with the greatest number of functions.

The internal organs

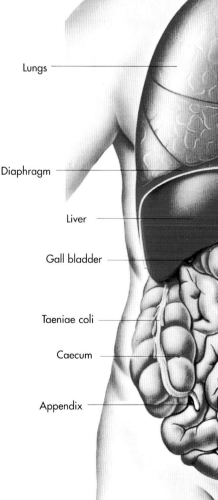

Epiglottis

Larynx

Trachea

Lungs

Diaphragm

Liver

Gall bladder

Taeniae coli

Caecum

Appendix

FACT FILE

When a doctor replaces a damaged organ with a healthy one from a donor, the operation is called a transplant. Nowadays the heart, liver, kidneys and lungs can all be transplanted.

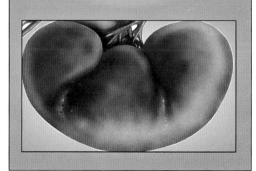

WHAT IS INSIDE AN ANIMAL CELL?

All living things, plant and animal, are made from cells. These cells consist mostly of a watery jelly-like material called cytoplasm. Each cell is held together by a very thin flexible membrane, rather like a balloon filled with water. Inside the cell the cytoplasm is organized into special areas called organelles. These control the functioning of the cell, for example, the production of essential substances called proteins. Tiny organelles called mitochondria use oxygen to break down food and release the energy that powers the cell. An area called the nucleus contains 46 thread-like chromosomes that control the working of the cell. Some cells, such as those lining the intestines, only live for a few days, while other nerve cells within the brain can survive throughout your entire life.

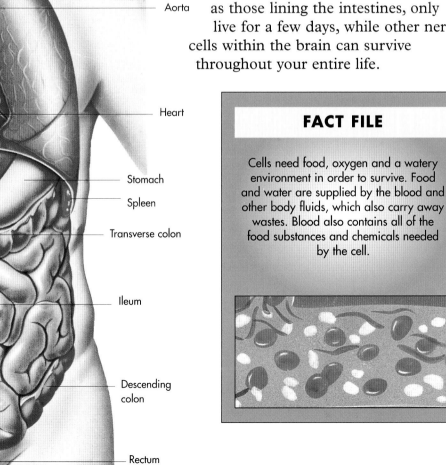

Hyoid bone

Thyroid gland

Aorta

Heart

Stomach

Spleen

Transverse colon

Ileum

Descending colon

Rectum

FACT FILE

Cells need food, oxygen and a watery environment in order to survive. Food and water are supplied by the blood and other body fluids, which also carry away wastes. Blood also contains all of the food substances and chemicals needed by the cell.

WHAT IS DNA?

DNA (short for deoxyribonucleic acid) is the basic unit of control of human life. It is a highly complex substance formed from a chain of chemical units called nucleotides. All the instructions for growing a new human being are coded into the DNA molecule. It is shaped like a ladder twisted into a spiral. The two long upright strands are joined by a series of rungs of pairs of amino acids, which can only join together in a limited number of ways. The pattern in which these pairs appear is the code built into the DNA molecule, and groups of these connections form genes. Each DNA molecule is built up of between 100,000 to 10 million atoms. There are 46 chromosomes in the full human set: 23 came from the mother and were in the egg cell, and 23 came from the father in the sperm cell. Every time a cell divides, each piece of DNA in every chromosome is copied.

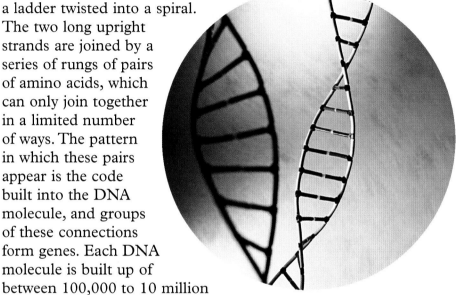

Model of DNA

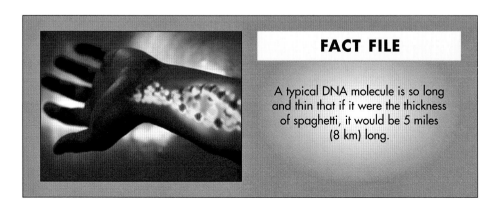

FACT FILE

A typical DNA molecule is so long and thin that if it were the thickness of spaghetti, it would be 5 miles (8 km) long.

WHAT DETERMINES EYE PIGMENT?

FACT FILE

A fly can pick out 200 images each second. It sees a movie or TV program as a series of still pictures. Maybe this is why flies don't watch television!

There is more than one gene for eye pigment, as shown in the illustration *below*, but brown is always dominant over blue. Two people, one with two genes for brown eyes, the other with two genes for blue eyes (A), will have children who all have brown eyes. However, if two brown-eyed parents (B) carry the heterozygous recessive blue gene they will have one blue-eyed child for every three brown-eyed children.

Dominant eye genes

A   B

WHAT IS BONE MADE FROM?

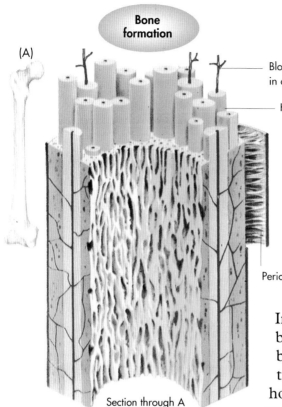

Bone formation

(A)

Blood and lymph vessels in central canal

Haversian system

Periosteum

Section through A

A typical bone (A) is actually made of two types of bony tissue. On the outside is a type of 'skin' called the periosteum. Below this is a thin layer of thick, dense, 'solid' bone. It is known as hard or compact bony tissue. Inside this, and forming the bulk of the middle of the bone, is a different bony tissue, more like a sponge or honeycomb. It has gaps and spaces, and it is called spongy, or alveolar, bony tissue. It is much lighter than the outer compact bone, and the spaces are filled with blood vessels, and jelly-like bone marrow for making new blood cells.

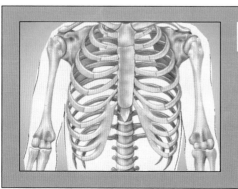

FACT FILE

There are 206 bones in the average body. However, there are a few people who have more, such as an extra pair of ribs, making 13 pairs instead of 12 and therefore 208 bones in total.

WHAT IS CORONARY CIRCULATION?

Coronary circulation

Aorta

Left coronary artery

Right coronary artery

Coronary vein

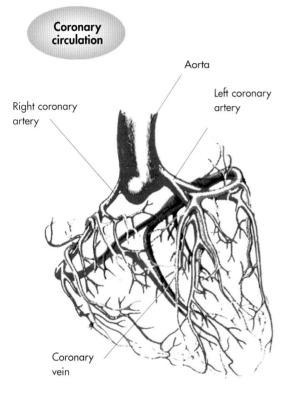

FACT FILE

Sometimes the heart valves become stiff or leaky. They can be replaced by valves made from tissue taken from an animal, or by artificial valves made of metal and plastic.

Main veins from body

Aorta and main arteries to body

Pulmonary arteries to lungs

Coronary circulation is part of the systemic circulatory system that supplies blood to and provides drainage from the tissues of the heart. In the human heart, two coronary arteries arise from the aorta just beyond the semilunar valves; during diastole (when the heart's chambers dilute and fill with blood) the increased aortic pressure above the valves forces blood into the coronary arteries and then into the musculature of the heart. Deoxygenated blood is returned to the chambers of the heart via coronary veins and then drained into the right ventricle below the tricuspid valve.

The heart normally extracts 70 to 75 percent of the available oxygen from the blood in coronary circulation, which is much more than the amount extracted by other organs from their circulations. Obstruction of a coronary artery, depriving the heart tissue of oxygen-rich blood, leads to death of part of the heart muscle in severe cases.

45

WHAT IS BLOOD MADE FROM?

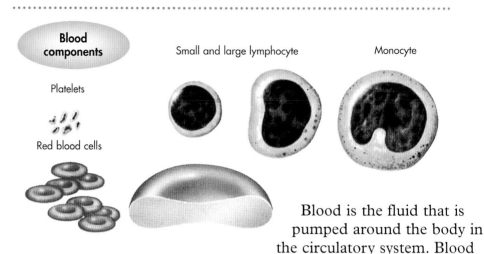

Blood components

Small and large lymphocyte

Monocyte

Platelets

Red blood cells

Blood is the fluid that is pumped around the body in the circulatory system. Blood carries oxygen, which it picks up in the lungs. It distributes this oxygen to all body parts, since every body cell needs a regular supply of oxygen to stay alive. Blood is made up of many components and has many functions. It consists of a yellow fluid, called plasma, in which red and white blood corpuscles and platelets are suspended. The capillaries allow fluid to escape from the blood. The cells and large proteins are left in the vessel and this fluid can now become the interstitial fluid (a background fluid that acts as an active support). This will either return to the capillary or join the lymphatic system. Blood amounts to about one-third of the total interstitial fluid.

The red and white blood cells are formed in the bone marrow. The plasma occupies about 55 percent of the blood volume. It is 90 percent water, 7 percent proteins, with the remaining 3 percent made up of small molecules.

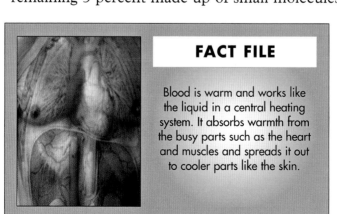

FACT FILE

Blood is warm and works like the liquid in a central heating system. It absorbs warmth from the busy parts such as the heart and muscles and spreads it out to cooler parts like the skin.

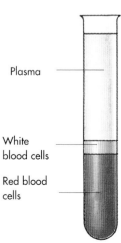

Plasma

White blood cells

Red blood cells

WHAT IS BLOOD CLOTTING?

When you cut yourself, the blood clots to prevent the wound from bleeding. Clotting is caused by substances in the blood. Together with small particles called platelets, these substances produce masses of fine mesh when they are exposed to air. They block the wound and prevent more blood loss. New cells grow rapidly into the wound, replacing the damaged tissue. Soon the clotted material, called a scab, falls off and clean, new skin is revealed underneath.

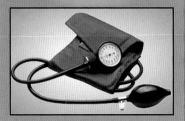

TELL ME WHAT : THE HUMAN BODY

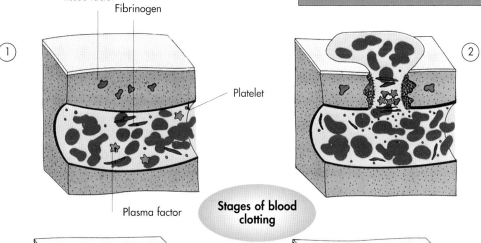

Tissue factor

Fibrinogen

① ②

Platelet

Plasma factor

Stages of blood clotting

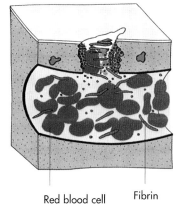

③

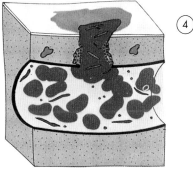

④

Red blood cell   Fibrin

47

WHAT IS LYMPH?

Your body's main attack force is called the lymph system. Like the blood system, it is a set of vessels which carry liquid round the body. This liquid is called lymph. Lymph contains special white blood cells called lymphocytes. These can make substances called antibodies which fight germs and cope with poisons. It works in the following way: The fluid passes out of the capillary (**1**) and either into the vein or into the smallest, thin-walled lymph vessel (**2**). These vessels join together to form large channels and finally reach the thoracic duct running next to the descending aorta. This duct joins one of the main branches of the superior vena cava (**5**). Valves (**3**) keep lymph flowing in one direction. Lymph glands (**4**) are found throughout the body and at places where lymph vessels unite (**6**).

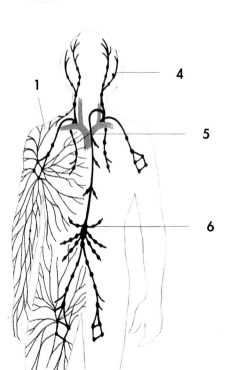

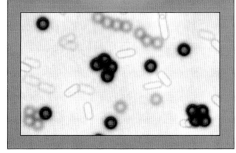

FACT FILE

Bacteria are tiny, single-celled organisms. They can measure as little as 0.001mm across and they can only be seen under a microscope. There are many different sorts of bacteria, and most of them are harmless.

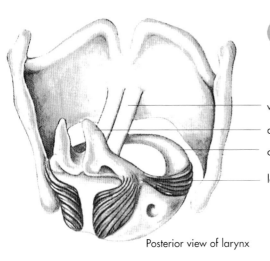

Speech and voice mechanism

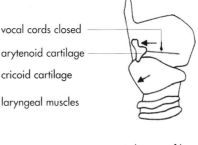

vocal cords closed

arytenoid cartilage

cricoid cartilage

laryngeal muscles

Side view of larynx

Posterior view of larynx

WHAT IS THE PURPOSE OF OUR VOICE BOX?

We make sounds when air is forced through our vocal cords, making them vibrate. The vocal cords are two rubbery bands of cartilage inside the larynx. This body part is called the voice box. It is at the top of the windpipe and it shows up on the outside of the throat as a lump called the Adam's apple.

The muscles of the larynx can alter the shape of the cords to produce different sounds. The cords produce low-pitched sounds when they are close together, and high-pitched sounds when they are far apart. The harder the air is forced out, the louder the sounds you make. You use the muscles of your throat, mouth and lips to form the sounds into words.

FACT FILE

At the age of puberty a boy's voice 'breaks'. The larynx enlarges, due to the effect of the male hormone, testosterone, and the vocal cords become longer. This means that the boy now has a lower bass range.

WHAT IS INSIDE THE LUNGS?

You have two lungs, one in each side of your chest, enclosed by an airtight box. Your ribs and the muscles that join them form the box, together with a tough sheet of muscle called the diaphragm.

Inside the lungs are tiny air sacs called alveoli, surrounded by capillaries. The walls of the alveoli and capillaries are so thin that oxygen and carbon dioxide can pass through them. The alveoli of an adult have a total surface area of $70\,m^2$, and the whole breathing apparatus is designed to bring fresh air as close as possible to the blood. Your lungs fill with air when you breathe in, and empty when you breathe out. They go up and down rather like balloons, but they aren't just hollow bags. They are spongy organs made up of tightly packed tissue, nerves and blood vessels.

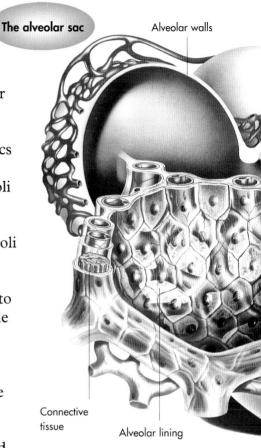

The alveolar sac

Alveolar walls

Connective tissue

Alveolar lining

FACT FILE

Underwater animals, like fish, have breathing organs called gills instead of lungs. These can take in oxygen from the water. To enable us to breathe underwater we need an oxygen tank, because if our lungs filled with water we would drown.

WHAT IS BRONCHITIS?

Pulmonary venules

Lymph vessels

Terminal bronchiole

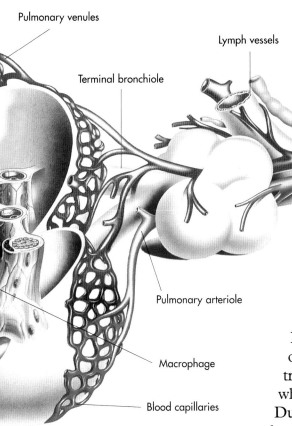

Pulmonary arteriole

Macrophage

Blood capillaries

Bronchitis is an inflammation
of all or part of the bronchial
tree (the bronchi), through
which air passes into the lungs.
During the passage through the
bronchi, microorganisms and
other foreign bodies are removed
from the air by tiny hairlike structures called cilia, which project from the
cells that line the bronchial wall. These cilia have a wavelike motion and
sweep the foreign material upward toward the trachea and larynx.
Because of this irritation a thick mucus is produced by glands in the
bronchial wall and aid in the elimination of the foreign material. Such
material and the secreted mucus stimulate nerve endings in the bronchial
wall and cause you to cough in an effort to expel the foreign material.

Acute bronchitis is caused by any of a great number of agents and not
as a specific disease. It is most frequently caused by viruses responsible
for upper respiratory infections and is, therefore, often part of what is
called the common cold.

TELL ME WHAT : THE HUMAN BODY

WHAT IS INSULIN?

Insulin is a hormone produced by the pancreas. The purpose of insulin is to keep the level of sugar in the blood down to normal levels.

If the level of sugar in the blood begins to rise above certain limits, the Islets of Langerhans respond by releasing insulin into the bloodstream. The insulin then acts to oppose the effects of hormones such as cortisone and adrenalin, both of which raise the level of sugar in the blood. The insulin exerts its effect by allowing sugar to pass from the bloodstream into the body's cells to be used as a fuel.

FACT FILE

At least 21 different organs – such as hearts, livers and kidneys – can now be successfully transplanted into patients. Kidneys are the most common organs to be transplanted; they remove waste products from the blood stream.

Cross-section of a kidney

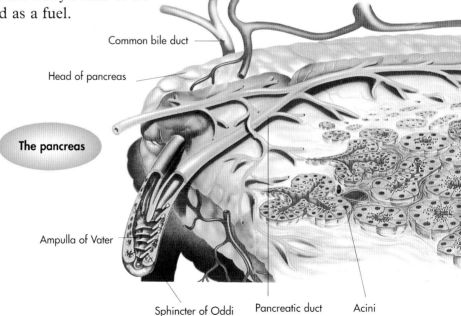

Common bile duct

Head of pancreas

The pancreas

Ampulla of Vater

Sphincter of Oddi

Pancreatic duct

Acini

WHAT IS THE PANCREAS?

The pancreas is one of the largest glands in the body and it is really two glands in one. Almost all of its cells are concerned with secretion. The pancreas lies across the upper part of the abdomen in front of the spine and on top of the aorta and the vena cava (the body's main artery and vein). The duodenum is wrapped round the head of the pancreas. The basic structures in the pancreas are the acini, which are collections of secreting cells around the end of a small duct. Each duct joins up with ducts from other acini until all of them eventually connect with the main duct running down the middle of the pancreas. The Islets of Langerhans are cells that are responsible for the secretion of insulin, which is needed by the body for the constant control of its sugar level. The Islets also produce a hormone called glucagon whose job it is to raise the level of sugar in the blood, rather than lowering it. The pancreas also plays an important part in digestion as it secretes digestive enzymes into the small intestine.

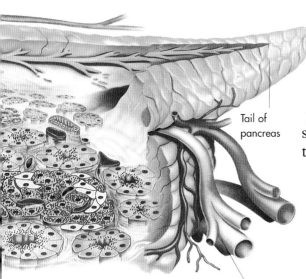

Tail of pancreas

Islets of Langerhans

Mesenteric veins

TELL ME WHAT : THE HUMAN BODY

53

WHAT DOES OUR DIGESTIVE SYSTEM DO?

Everything you eat has to be chopped up and broken down before the nutrients or goodness in it can be taken into your blood and used by your body cells to make energy. This chopping up and breaking down takes place in your digestive system, or gut.

Digestion begins with the first bite. In your mouth the food is chopped up and chewed by your teeth and mixed with saliva. Your tongue pushes and kneads the food into a ball. This ball of food is then pushed down a short tube called the oesophagus to your stomach. The food leaves your stomach a little at a time and goes into your small intestine. This is where most of the digestion takes place. Undigested food continues on to the large intestine, where water is taken from it, before travelling to the last part of your intestine, the rectum.

duodenum

stomach

pancreas

hepatic portal vein

colon

ileum

appendix

rectum

anus

The digestive tract

FACT FILE

Your digestive system is a long tube which begins at your mouth and ends at your anus. In adults it is about 9 m long! Food can take anything from 10 to 20 hours to pass through it.

WHAT IS INSIDE THE STOMACH?

If you did not have a stomach you could not eat just two or three main meals each day. You would have to eat lots of tiny ones much more frequently. The stomach is like a stretchy storage bag for food. It expands to hold a whole meal. Then the layers of muscle in its walls contract to make it squeeze, first one way, then the other. Meanwhile, tiny glands in the stomach lining release their digestive chemicals, including powerful food-corroding acids and strong nutrient-splitting enzymes. Under this combined physical and chemical attack, after a few hours the food has become a mushy, part-digested soup. Around two to four hours after arriving in your stomach, the part-digested soup begins to leave. Small amounts trickle regularly from the stomach into the next section of the digestive tract – the small intestine.

FACT FILE

A normal X-ray photograph does not reveal the parts of the digestive system. However, a substance called barium shows up clearly on X-rays as a white area. If swallowed, this 'barium meal' can reveal problems such as ulcers, growths and blockages.

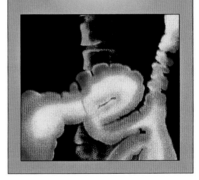

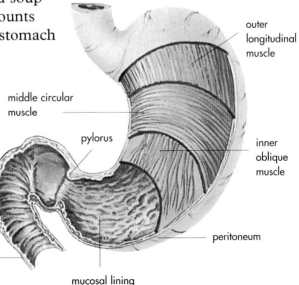

The stomach

outer longitudinal muscle

middle circular muscle

pylorus

inner oblique muscle

duodenum

peritoneum

mucosal lining

WHAT IS THE ROLE OF THE LIVER?

The liver is one of the body's busiest parts. It does not squirm about or move, like the stomach, intestines, heart, or muscles. Its activities are invisible. The liver is the body's largest inner organ, weighing about 0.90 -1.36 kg (2-3 lbs), and fills the top part of the abdomen, especially on the right side. It has at least 500 known jobs in body chemistry, all different and important.

The liver has a special blood vessel to it – the hepatic portal vein. This does not come directly from the heart, but carries blood that has been to the stomach, intestines, and spleen. This blood is rich in nutrients, which provide the body with its energy and raw materials. The liver processes many of the nutrients brought to it by the blood. It stores others, especially glucose sugar, minerals such as iron, and vitamins such as B12. It also detoxifies possible harmful substances.

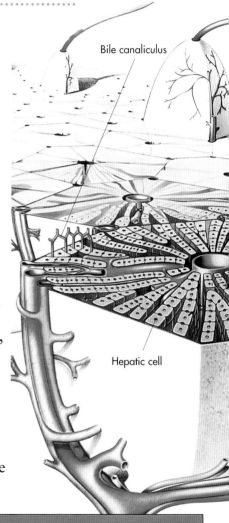

Bile canaliculus

Hepatic cell

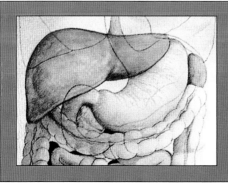

FACT FILE

Cirrhosis of the liver is an irreversible chronic disease characterized by the replacement of functioning liver tissue with bands and lumps of scar tissue. This disease is often associated with drinking too much alcohol.

WHAT IS BILE?

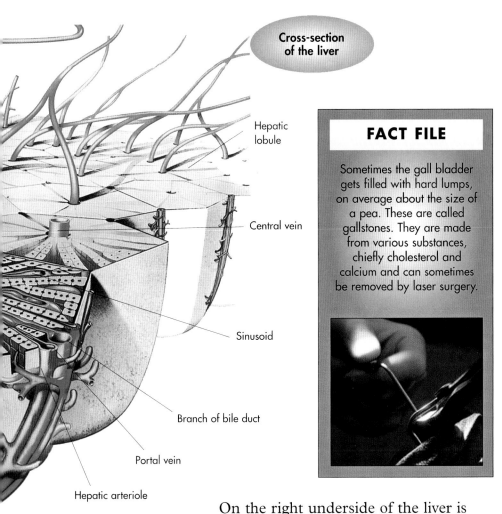

Cross-section of the liver

Hepatic lobule

Central vein

Sinusoid

Branch of bile duct

Portal vein

Hepatic arteriole

FACT FILE

Sometimes the gall bladder gets filled with hard lumps, on average about the size of a pea. These are called gallstones. They are made from various substances, chiefly cholesterol and calcium and can sometimes be removed by laser surgery.

On the right underside of the liver is the gall bladder. It is a small bag that contains a yellowish fluid called bile. Bile is a solution of cholesterol, bile salts and pigments. The liver makes up to a full quart of bile every day. Some of this stays in the liver and some in the gall bladder – that is until you have a meal. Then bile flows from the gall bladder and liver to a main tube, called the common bile duct, which empties into the small intestine. Bile is a waste product from the liver, but it also helps with digestion. The mineral salts in it break up, or emulsify, fatty foods in the intestine by turning the fats into tiny droplets.

WHAT IS THE ROLE OF THE KIDNEYS?

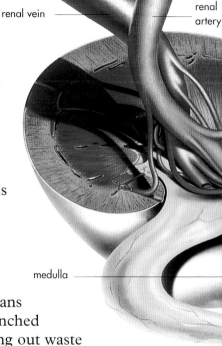

Cross-section of the kidneys

renal vein

renal artery

medulla

capsule of tough fibrous tissue

Our bodies' cells 'burn' nutrients and oxygen to make energy to live and grow, in much the same way that wood and other materials are burnt to produce another sort of energy – heat. But just as fires produce waste gases and ash, so the 'burning' that takes place in our body cells also creates waste products. These must be removed, or they would poison us.

The removal of these waste materials is known as excretion, and the body's main organs of excretion are the kidneys. You have two kidneys positioned in the small of your back, one on either side of your backbone. They look like large reddish-brown beans and each one is about the size of a clenched fist. Kidneys clean the blood by filtering out waste materials and straining off any water the body doesn't need. This liquid waste is called urine. It is stored in your bladder and leaves your body when you go to the toilet.

FACT FILE

We lose around 5 pints (3 ltr) of water a day through our skin as sweat, and in our breath and urine. We also get rid of extra salt in sweat, and we expel waste carbon dioxide gas when we breathe out.

WHAT IS DIALYSIS?

If the kidneys become diseased and stop working, it is necessary to use a kidney machine to remove waste products from the blood. This machine process is called dialysis. It involves pumping blood from a tube in the person's arm into thin tubing that runs through a tank of sterile liquid. Waste passes through the blood through the walls of the tubing, and the cleaned blood is returned to the body. The dialysis machine works the same way as the two main blood vessels running to and from the kidneys. One tube takes the unfiltered blood from the body (like the renal artery), while another tube takes the cleaned blood back into the body (like the renal vein). This process has to be done throughout the person's life, unless a new kidney can be provided in a transplant operation. Dialysis needs to be carried out frequently, several times a week, to stop wastes from building up to a dangerous level.

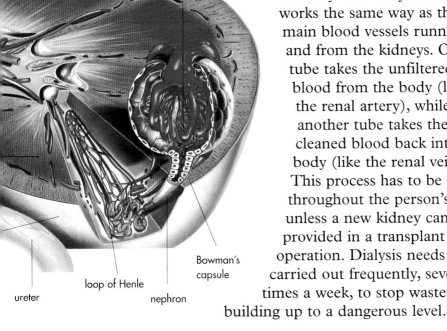

cortex
arteriole
glomerulus
Bowman's capsule
loop of Henle
ureter
nephron

FACT FILE

The human body is made up of approximately 70 per cent water. It is therefore very important that we drink plenty of water every day.

WHAT ARE THE AREAS OF THE BRAIN CALLED?

Basically the brain can be divided into three different regions: hindbrain, midbrain and forebrain. Each of these regions is in turn divided into separate areas responsible for quite distinct functions, all intricately linked to other parts of the brain.

The largest structure in the hindbrain is called the cerebellum. The largest part of the entire brain is the cerebrum, which is located in the forebrain. It is more developed in humans than in any other animal. This is where the other parts of the brain send incoming messages for decision. The cerebral cortex is the thick wrinkled layer of grey matter folded over the outside of the cerebrum. This part of the brain has become so highly developed in humans that it has had to fold over and over in order to fit inside the skull. Unfolded, it would cover an area 30 times as large as when folded.

FACT FILE

Shivering is governed by four mechanisms. The hypothalamus, at the base of the brain, senses that the temperature is too low and sends messages to the thyroid gland, telling it to speed up the metabolic rate. The body muscles then alternately contract and relax rapidly, thus producing heat. The nerves then send messages to the skin and the skin pores narrow, ensuring that the heat is conserved within the body.

The human brain

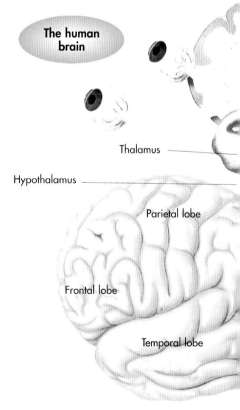

Thalamus

Hypothalamus

Parietal lobe

Frontal lobe

Temporal lobe

WHAT ARE THE THREE MAIN FUNCTIONS OF THE BRAIN?

The brain is the body's control centre. It keeps the body working smoothly and it looks after thoughts, feelings and memory.

Different parts of the brain have different jobs to do. The largest part is called the cerebrum, or forebrain. It looks like a huge half-walnut. The cerebrum's main job is to sort out and respond to messages sent to it from the senses. It also stores information, as memory, and it thinks. Messages from the senses are managed by the cerebrum's sensory area, while the motor area controls the muscles. Thinking, memory and speech are managed by the parts known as the association areas. The cerebellum (or hindbrain) is below the cerebrum. It works with the cerebrum's motor area to ensure that the muscles function smoothly.

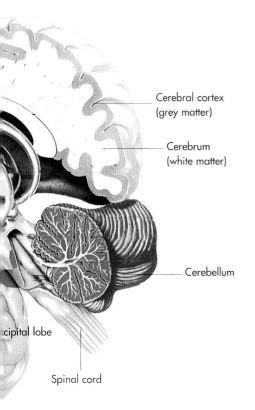

Cerebral cortex
(grey matter)

Cerebrum
(white matter)

Cerebellum

cipital lobe

Spinal cord

FACT FILE

Although we have invented computers that can work out millions of different things in seconds, our brains can still outwork and outsmart them! Our brains control our bodies by sending out billions of tiny electrical signals every second.

WHAT IS THE RETINA?

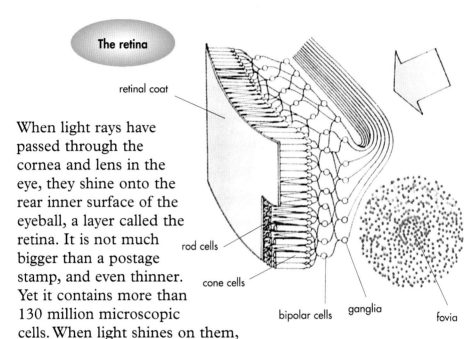

The retina

retinal coat

rod cells

cone cells

bipolar cells

ganglia

fovia

When light rays have passed through the cornea and lens in the eye, they shine onto the rear inner surface of the eyeball, a layer called the retina. It is not much bigger than a postage stamp, and even thinner. Yet it contains more than 130 million microscopic cells. When light shines on them, they generate nerve signals – that is, they are light sensitive. There are two types of light sensitive cells in the retina, named after their shapes – rods and cones. There are about 125 million rods and they all respond to all types of light, regardless of whether it is white, red, blue, green, or yellow. Rods work in very weak light, so they help the eye to see in dim conditions. The other type of light-sensitive cell is the cone. There are about 7 million of them in the retina, clustered mainly around the back, opposite the lens.

FACT FILE

The image of the world 'lingers' for a fraction of a second on the retina and in the brain. This means if images change very fast, each merges or blurs into the next, so we see them as one smooth, continuous moving scene.

WHAT MAKES THE EYEBALL MOVE?

Eye muscles (left eye)

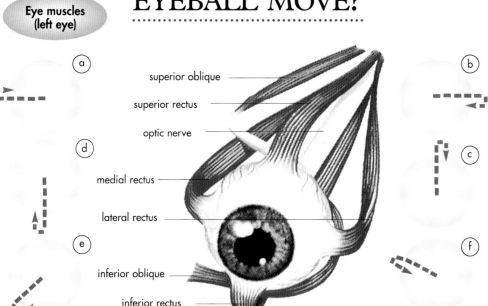

(a)

(b)

superior oblique

superior rectus

optic nerve

(d)

(c)

medial rectus

lateral rectus

(e)

(f)

inferior oblique

inferior rectus

There are six muscles to control the movements of each eye. Muscle (a) swivels it away from the nose; (b) towards the nose; (c) rotates it upwards; (d) downwards; (e) moves it down and outwards and (f) moves it upwards and outwards. All these movements are coordinated in the brain. If the lateral rectus muscle in one eye contracts, the medial rectus of the other will contract to a similar extent. The superior recti work together to pull the eyes back and also to look up. The inferior recti make the eyes look down. The superior oblique muscles rotate the eye downwards and outwards and the inferior oblique upwards and outwards.

FACT FILE

The eyes are the body's windows on the world and need special protection. Every second or so the eyelids blink and sweep tear fluid across the eye washing away dust and germs. Eyebrows stop water from dripping down into the eyes. Eyelashes help to keep out the dust.

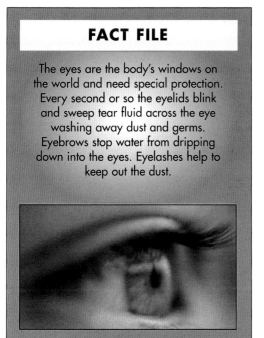

WHAT IS PUPIL REFLEX?

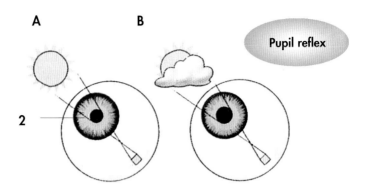

A B

Pupil reflex

2

The muscles contract to make the pupil smaller in bright conditions. This stops too much light getting into the eye and damaging its delicate inner parts. The retina is very sensitive to light. Too much light (**A**) distorts what we see and is dazzling. The pupils vary in size and thus reduce or increase the amount of light entering the eye. Bright light causes a reflex nervous reaction, controlled by areas in the midbrain. The circular pupillary muscle (**1**) in both irises contracts and the radial strands (**2**) extend, thus narrowing the diameter.

Poor light (**B**) will make both pupils dilate, allowing sufficient light to stimulate the cells in the retina (**3**).

FACT FILE

Did you know that the human eye is so sensitive that a person sitting on top of a hill on a moonless night could see a match being struck up to 80 km away.

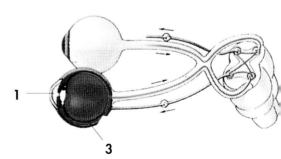

1

3

WHAT IS THE FOCUSING MECHANISM IN THE EYE?

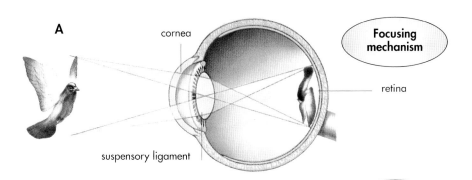

A

cornea

Focusing mechanism

retina

suspensory ligament

B

lens

ciliary muscle

The lens of the eye is shaped like the lens in a camera and does a similar job. It adds to the focusing power of the cornea and makes fine adjustments, depending on whether the object is near or far away. The eye's lens is slightly elastic and focuses by changing shape. After the lens, the light rays go through the clear jelly in the middle of the eye ball to the retina. In distant vision (A) the muscles relax and the ligaments pull the lens into a disc shape. Close vision (B) requires a more circular lens, so the muscles constrict and the ligaments relax.

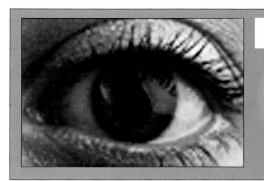

FACT FILE

Why do we have two eyes? Close one eye. Hold a pencil in one hand. Stretch out your arm in front of you and try to touch something. Can you do it? Two eyes working together help you to see how close things really are.

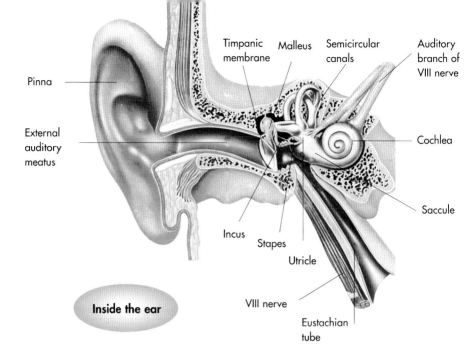

Pinna

Timpanic membrane

Malleus

Semicircular canals

Auditory branch of VIII nerve

External auditory meatus

Cochlea

Incus

Stapes

Utricle

Saccule

Inside the ear

VIII nerve

Eustachian tube

WHAT IS INSIDE THE EAR?

Hearing involves much more than the ears on the side of your head. These are the outer ears or ear flaps, made of skin-covered cartilage. The ear is actually made up of three parts. The outer ear collects sound waves, which are vibrations in the air. The middle ear turns them into vibrations in solids – the ear drum and tiny bones. The inner ear changes them into vibrations in fluid, and then into electrical nerve signals. The inner ear also gives us our sense of balance. The middle and inner ears are protected from knocks by skull bones. The hairs and waxy lining of the outer ear canal gather and remove dust and germs.

FACT FILE

When you go up in a lift or fly in a plane, your ears may pop as the air inside them expands. If this did not happen, your eardrum would burst.

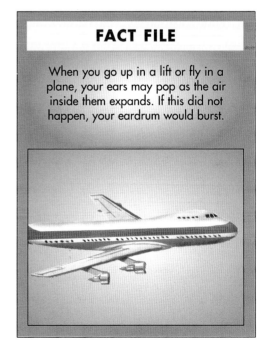

WHAT IS THE COCHLEA?

FACT FILE

Loud noises make the eardrum tighten, pulling the stirrup bone away from the cochlea in order to protect the inner ear. Very loud noises can tear the eardrum and cause deafness.

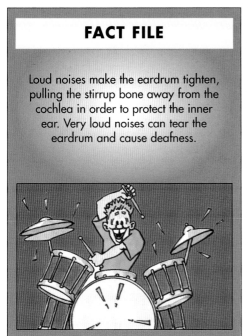

The hearing portion is situated at one end of the ear chamber and forms a coil rather like the shell of a snail. It is called the cochlea and throughout its length runs a thin membrane called the basilar membrane which supplies thousands of tiny nerve threads to the cochlea nerve. Changes in the pitch or loudness of sounds are sensed by tiny hairs through which pressure waves travel. When sounds travel into the ear, they make the eardrum inside vibrate, or shake. The vibrations pass along a chain of tiny bones called the hammer, anvil and stirrup, and are made louder before passing into the cochlea. The vibrations are then picked up by nerve endings inside the cochlea, and changed into messages to send to the brain.

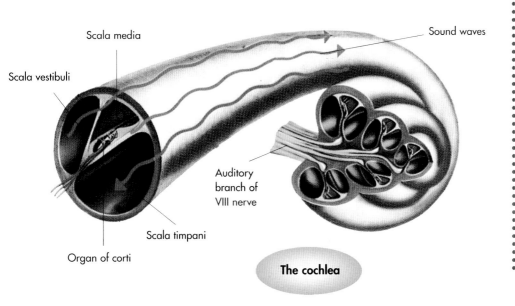

Scala media

Scala vestibuli

Sound waves

Auditory branch of VIII nerve

Scala timpani

Organ of corti

The cochlea

WHAT CONTROLS OUR BALANCE?

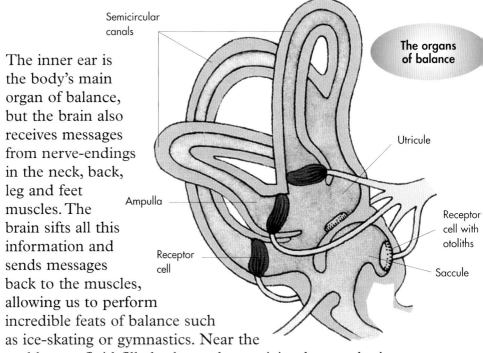

Semicircular canals

The organs of balance

Utricule

Ampulla

Receptor cell with otoliths

Receptor cell

Saccule

The inner ear is the body's main organ of balance, but the brain also receives messages from nerve-endings in the neck, back, leg and feet muscles. The brain sifts all this information and sends messages back to the muscles, allowing us to perform incredible feats of balance such as ice-skating or gymnastics. Near the cochlea are fluid-filled tubes – the semicircular canals. As your head moves about, the fluid inside each canal swishes to and fro. When the body moves, the fluid causes hairs in a jelly-like mass to bend. These are connected to the vestibular nerve, which alerts the brain to re-balance the body.

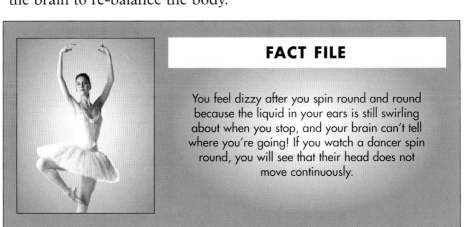

FACT FILE

You feel dizzy after you spin round and round because the liquid in your ears is still swirling about when you stop, and your brain can't tell where you're going! If you watch a dancer spin round, you will see that their head does not move continuously.

WHAT CONTROLS OUR TEMPERATURE?

FACT FILE

Body movements can also be homeostatic. A hot person may spread out arms and legs to increase heat loss; a cold person curls up to reduce the areas of the body losing warmth.

The name for 'constancy of the internal environment' is homeostasis. The body must regulate many body systems and processes to keep inner conditions stable. The temperature nucleus in the hypothalamus controls heat loss and production by the body through the skin. Overheating (**A**) causes an increased blood flow from the blood vessels (**1**), to radiate heat and causes sweating through the sweat glands (**2**), to lose heat. A fall in body temperature (**B**) constricts the surface blood vessels, stops sweating and makes the erector muscles (**3**) contract, causing the hairs (**4**) to stand on end, trapping air as an insulating layer. Additional heat can be produced by shivering.

Temperature control

A

2

1

B

3

4

WHAT IS SKIN?

Skin covers your body in a pastry-thin layer, in most parts around 2 mm thick.
It is thicker on the soles of your feet and the palms of your hands, around 3 mm. It is both waterproof and stretchy, and it protects you from the outside world by helping to keep out harmful things like dirt and germs.

Skin has two main layers. The protective outer layer is called the epidermis. The skin you can see on your body is the top of the epidermis, which is made up of dead cells. New cells are made at the bottom of the epidermis and gradually push their way upwards. The inner layer of the skin is called the dermis. The sensory receptors for touch, heat, cold, pressure and pain are here, as well as the nerve-endings that pick up information and carry it to the brain. The dermis is also where sweat is made and hair grows.

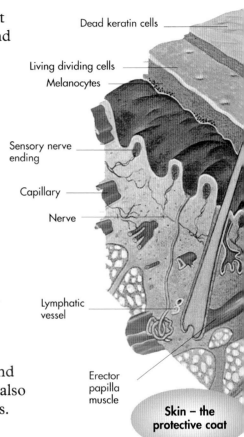

Dead keratin cells

Living dividing cells

Melanocytes

Sensory nerve ending

Capillary

Nerve

Lymphatic vessel

Erector papilla muscle

Skin – the protective coat

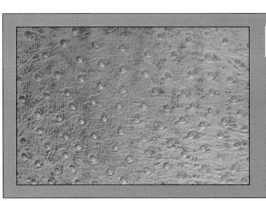

FACT FILE

Each hair on your body has a tiny erector muscle. When you are cold these muscles contract to make the hairs stand up, trapping warm air between them and giving you goosebumps.

WHAT IS SENSATION?

Your skin is a huge sense organ with thousands of sensory receptors. Skin receptors are not only sensitive to touch and texture – telling you whether something is smooth or furry, for example. There are also receptors that respond to heat, and ones that respond to cold. Yet others tell you when something is putting pressure on your skin.

Some skin receptors are sensitive to all four. They are called free nerve-endings and they are thought to send out pain signals if messages from touch, heat, cold or pressure receptors are too strong.

There are free nerve-endings wrapped around the hairs in your skin, sensitive to each hair's slightest movement. Some areas of the skin are densely packed with nerve endings, as in the finger-tips, while others, as on the back, have comparatively few.

Sweat gland duct pore

Hair

Epidermis

Dermis

Subcutaneous layer

Hair follicle

Sweat gland

Fat cells

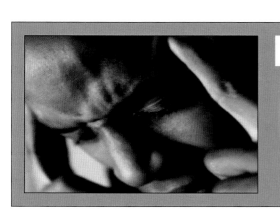

FACT FILE

You have other senses beside the five main ones, including those of balance, hunger and thirst. Your sense of pain is very important – it warns you when your body is hurt or in danger.

THE NATURAL

WORLD

CONTENTS

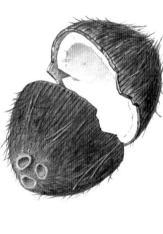

WHAT ARE MAMMALS?

Mammals are vertebrate animals who nourish their young with milk. All mammals and birds are warm-blooded. Most mammals have hair on their bodies which moults to be thin in the summer and thick in the winter. They also have a big brain inside their alert head, which enables them to learn quickly from experience, and retain memory so that they can undertake quite complicated tasks such as

Stoat

finding a safe home and food. They have a strong internal skeleton of bones, including toes on four limbs, plus a tail which, like the ears, can be very obvious. They can control their body heat over a wide range of weather conditions. Mammals have adapted to life in woodland, rivers, estuaries, seas, land, air, mountains and even the desert.

Rabbit

FACT FILE

The female of any mammal, like the polecat *below*, has the vital role of rearing the next generation. A typical feature is her milk or mammary glands with which to feed her young (hence the name 'mammal').

WHAT IS THE ADVANTAGE OF BEING WARM-BLOODED?

A warm-blooded animal is an animal that almost always has about the same body temperature, regardless of the temperature of its surroundings. Birds and mammals, including human beings, are warm-blooded animals. Nearly all other kinds of animals are cold-blooded. The body of a warm-blooded animal produces heat by burning food. Shivering and physical activity also generate body heat. Young warm-blooded animals and some adult small mammals have heat-producing organs, called brown fat, on their neck, chest, and back. A layer of fat beneath the skin, plus a covering of hair, fur, or feathers, helps keep a warm-blooded animal warm. The body becomes cooler by such means as panting and sweating.

Seal

FACT FILE

Some warm-blooded animals need to hibernate during cold spells to reduce their need for food and to protect themselves from the cold. These include mammals such as bats, chipmunks, hamsters, squirrels, hedgehogs, lemurs and marmots.

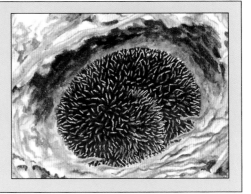

WHAT IS A MARSUPIAL?

Opossum

A marsupial is a mammal whose young are born in an extremely immature state. The newborn undergoes most of its development attached to one of its mother's nipples and nourished by her milk. Females of most marsupials have a pouch, called the marsupium, which protects the babies.

There are about 270 species of marsupials, all of which live in either the Americas or Australasia. They include kangaroos, koalas and opossums. Kangaroos are the largest marsupials – most male red kangaroos stand about 1.8 m (6 ft) tall. The smallest marsupials are the shrew-like ningauis, weighing only about 3 grams. Marsupials inhabit many different environments including forests, plains and deserts.

Kangaroo

FACT FILE

The young of tree-dwelling marsupials, such as koalas and opossums, cling to their mother's back after they have left the pouch. They remain there until they no longer need the mother's milk.

WHAT IS A REPTILE?

Lizard

A reptile is an air-breathing animal with a body structure comprising of traits from amphibians, birds and mammals. Reptiles are generally scaly and their eggs are fertilized internally. Living reptiles include crocodiles, tortoises and turtles, snakes and lizards. There are about 6,000 surviving species. Long ago there were many more kinds of reptile, such as the dinosaurs and the flying pterosaurs. Some reptiles lay eggs, but others give birth to live young which need no care from their parents.

FACT FILE

The tortoise and turtle are the only reptiles with a shell. They pull their head, legs, and tail into their shell, which serve as suits of armour. Few other backboned animals have such excellent natural protection.

Crocodile

WHAT IS AN INVERTEBRATE?

An invertebrate is an animal without a backbone, and they make up 97 percent of all animals. This group of animals includes all the arthropods such as spiders, insects and crustaceans. The remaining invertebrates are mainly soft-bodied animals, although many of them have shells. They include animals such as sponges, corals, shellfish, worms, sea urchins and starfish and many less familiar animals. One invertebrate, the octopus, has proved to be highly intelligent when studied in the laboratory. Experiments have shown that it can recognize shapes and can remember different experiences.

Stag beetles

Earthworm

Tarantula spider

FACT FILE

Assassin bugs are well named. They attack other insects and suck their body fluids. Caterpillars are a popular food because they have soft bodies and often no means of defence.

WHAT ARE MOLLUSCS?

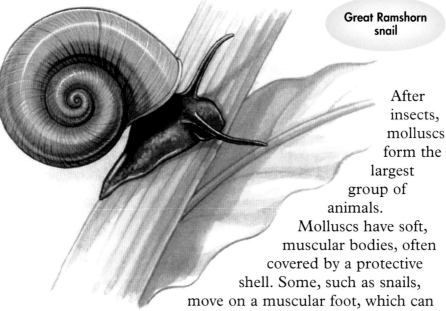

Great Ramshorn snail

After insects, molluscs form the largest group of animals.

Molluscs have soft, muscular bodies, often covered by a protective shell. Some, such as snails, move on a muscular foot, which can be withdrawn into the shell for protection. Other, sea-dwelling molluscs, such as squid and scallops, take in water and squirt it out to jet-propel themselves along. Many snails are an important food for fish, birds, and crustaceans, such as crayfish and lobsters. Many people consider the Helix garden snail, which is known as *escargot*, a great delicacy.

FACT FILE

Operculate snails are those with a plate which closes the mouth of the shell. When they are moving, the operculum can be seen attached to the foot.

Freshwater winkle

WHAT ARE ARTHROPODS?

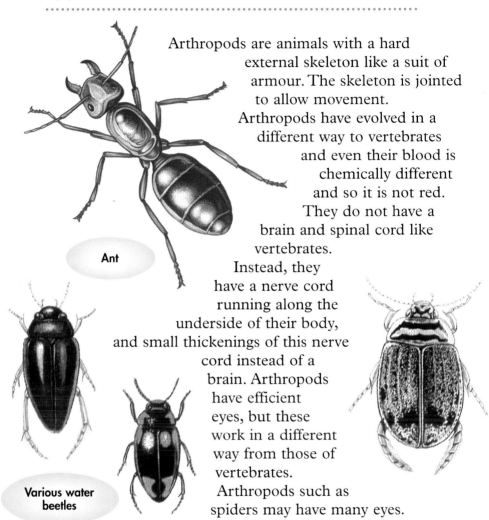

Arthropods are animals with a hard external skeleton like a suit of armour. The skeleton is jointed to allow movement.

Arthropods have evolved in a different way to vertebrates and even their blood is chemically different and so it is not red. They do not have a brain and spinal cord like vertebrates.

Instead, they have a nerve cord running along the underside of their body, and small thickenings of this nerve cord instead of a brain. Arthropods have efficient eyes, but these work in a different way from those of vertebrates.

Arthropods such as spiders may have many eyes.

Ant

Various water beetles

FACT FILE

The most important groups of arthropods are the following: (1) insects; (2) crustaceans (including this red-banded sea shrimp); (3) arachnids; (4) chilopods or centipedes; and (5) diplo-pods or millipedes.

WHAT IS A CRUSTACEAN?

Crab

FACT FILE

People in many parts of the world eat lobsters, crabs, shrimps and other crustaceans.

Crustaceans are aquatic arthropods such as crabs, lobsters and shrimps. They have a very tough, jointed external skeleton and jointed walking legs. Their body is divided into a region that contains most of the internal organs, covered by a shell called the carapace, and a muscular tail section that is usually folded under the body. Many crustaceans have powerful pincers that they use to capture and break up their prey, and to signal to others of their species. Crustaceans live in the sea and also freshwater habitats. Many small crustaceans feed on plankton. These crustaceans are then eaten by larger fish, and even whales. Crustaceans thus form an important link between the small food-producing organisms and the larger animals in the aquatic food chain.

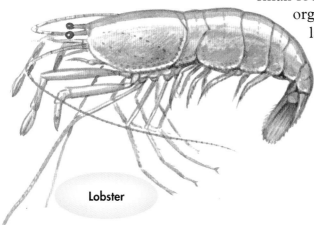

Lobster

WHAT ARE PARASITES?

Parasites are animals that live at the expense of other animals. They rob the host animal of nourishment and often cause it to become sick. However, in other types of relationships, different animals can help one another. Some hermit crabs place sea anemones on their shells, hiding under their protective stinging tentacles. At the same time, the sea anemone benefits because it shares the crab's food. Similarly, a species of shrimp digs a burrow that it shares with the small goby fish. The fish benefits from being able to hide in the burrow, while acting as a lookout to warn the shrimp of

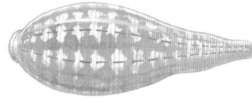

approaching predators. Most true parasites are very simple animals, because they do not need complicated organs to digest their food. Some parasites are simply a mass of reproductive organs.

Different types of leech

WHAT ARE MUSSELS?

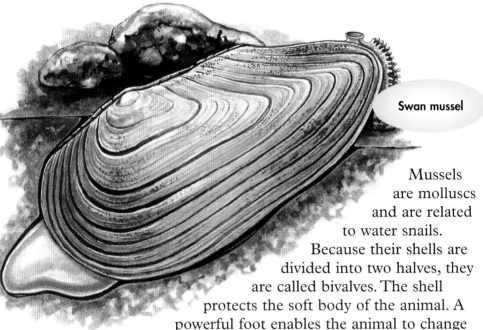

Swan mussel

Mussels
are molluscs
and are related
to water snails.
Because their shells are
divided into two halves, they
are called bivalves. The shell
protects the soft body of the animal. A
powerful foot enables the animal to change
its position. Mussels suck in water and extract the
oxygen and food that they require. There are both marine and
fresh water mussels and can be found worldwide. The marine
mussels prefer cool seas. Freshwater mussels, also known as naiads,
inhabit streams, lakes and ponds and there are around 1,000
known species. The shells are dark blue or dark greenish brown on
the outside, while on the inside they have a pearly appearance.
Mussels attach themselves to solid objects or to one another by
strands called byssus threads and often appear in dense clusters.

FACT FILE

The oystercatcher is a bird that feeds
largely on molluscs (such as mussels,
clams and oysters). They attack them as
the tide goes out, when their shells are
exposed and still partially open.

WHAT ARE PRIMATES?

Baby orang utan

There are about 180 different species of primate, most of them living in the tropical regions of the world. The most numerous primate is *Homo sapiens* – human beings. All primates have fairly large brains and forward-facing eyes that enable them to judge distances accurately. Instead of claws or hoofs, like other mammals, they have fingers and toes with soft, sensitive tips. They also have the ability to grasp with their fingers, thumbs and toes. The largest primate is the gorilla. A male can weigh up to 274 kg (605 lb). The smallest is the mouse lemur, which has a total body length of only 12.5 cm (6 ins).

FACT FILE

The gibbon is a small, man-like ape, found in Indo-Malayan forests. Gibbons, unlike the great apes, have elongated arms and hard, calloused skin on their buttocks. They have canine teeth and live in trees.

WHAT IS THE LARGEST ANIMAL IN THE WORLD?

FACT FILE

The largest land mammal is the African elephant which can weigh up to 7 tonnes (6.9 tons).

The blue whale is the largest animal that ever lived on Earth. It is also the loudest animal on Earth. These enormous mammals eat tiny organisms, like plankton and krill, which they sift through baleen (a horny substance attached to the upper jaw). They live in pods (small groups). These gray-blue whales have two blowholes and a 5-30 cm (2-14 in) thick layer of blubber. Blue whales are rorqual whales, whales that have pleated throat grooves that allow their throat to expand during the huge intake of water during filter feeding. Blue whales have 50-70 throat grooves that run from the throat to mid-body.

Blue whales

WHAT DO BIRDS EAT?

Gannet

Different species of birds have different diets, just as mammals do. Some are vegetarian, eating fruits and seeds. Others feed on insects and other invertebrates, such as worms. Birds' beaks are adapted to the kind of food they need. The beaks of meat-eaters are often hooked and sharp, ideal for tearing flesh from carcasses. Birds that search for food along the seashore or on mud banks often have long pointed beaks for burrowing into soft ground. It is fascinating to watch sea birds dive into the water. Gannets, for example, plunge in very spectacularly, head-first with folded wings, from up to 30 m or in a lower slanting dive. They disappear deep underwater, often with a splash of spray.

Other birds to watch feeding are the swift and the martin. These are all insect-eaters and feed on the wing. They can be seen circling above water to catch their prey.

FACT FILE

Bald eagles pluck fish out of the water with their talons, and sometimes they follow seabirds as a means of locating fish. Besides live fish, bald eagles prey on other birds, small mammals, snakes, turtles, and crabs.

Goldcrest

Falcon

WHAT ARE FEATHERS MADE OF?

Feathers consist of beta keratin, which is a form of protein, and are considered to have evolved from reptilian scales. Keratin can also be found in hair, hoofs and fingernails. Feathers are periodically moulted, and other keratinized structures such as the bill and claws may be moulted as well. Specialized nerve endings are present throughout the skin. There is a preen gland, which is located on the back just in front of the tail and secretes oil for grooming the feathers. This gland is most pronounced in aquatic birds, to ensure that their feathers are waterproof. The many different types of feathers are designed for insulation, flight, formation of body contours, display, and sensory reception. Unlike the hair of most mammals, feathers do not cover the entire skin surface of birds but are arranged in symmetrical tracts with areas of bare skin.

FACT FILE

Penguins have feathers but they cannot fly. They can swim at great speed using their wings as flippers to power them in the water.

WHAT IS A PECKING ORDER?

A living animal behaves constantly in order to survive, and all animals must solve the same basic problems. Animals do whatever they can to acquire all the energy they can use, and in this sense each is competing with all the others. Among animals that live in groups, one becomes the clear leader. In chickens, this means that one bird dominates all of the other birds.

The next one down in the 'pecking order' can dominate all except the leader, and so on, until the bird at the bottom of this process can be bullied by the entire flock. This can also be seen in families with dogs. The dog remains at the bottom of the pecking order and submits to the human members of the family.

FACT FILE

Dog fights do not usually cause too much damage. The loser will usually submit by lying down, which reduces the level of aggression in the dominant dog.

meat-eater

grazing animal

dung fertilizes the soil

nutrients are absorbed by the plant

WHAT IS THE FOOD CHAIN?

A food chain is a sequence that demonstrates how one organism forms the food for another. It begins with the simplest animals and plants, and continues until the top of the chain is reached. Humans or predator animals are often at the top of food chains.

Plants such as grass and trees are towards the bottom of the food chain. Grazing animals browse on these plants, and these animals are in turn eaten by predators such as lions. Their dung fertilizes the soil, encouraging the growth of more plants, so the food chain actually becomes a complete circle.

Primrose

WHAT IS A PLANT?

The evolutionary history of plants is recorded in fossils preserved in lowland or marine sediments and date back millions of years. A plant is an organism that uses light as a source of energy and to produce the food they need in order to live and grow. Plant cells have a tough outer wall made of a substance called cellulose, which makes the wall rigid. This explains why plants are able to move only very little, unlike animals whose cells have no rigid wall. Plants reproduce by passing their genetic information to descendants that resemble them. There are approximately 275,000 to 300,000 different species of plants, and new species are continuously being found, particularly from unexplored tropical areas of the world.

FACT FILE

Plants range in size from the giant Californian sequoias that reach 90 m (300 feet) or more in height to the tiny duck weeds, only a few inches in length. The picture shows duckweed being put into a fish tank. The small size of the plant is noticeable in comparison to the man's hand.

WHAT ARE LEAVES FOR?

FACT FILE

The shapes of leaves vary considerably. The edges may be smooth or jagged. The leaf blades may be undivided or divided as the maple leaf shown below.

Plants use a process called photo-synthesis in order to change sunlight into food. This process takes place mostly in the leaves of a plant. Leaves are large and flattened so that a large area of chlorophyll is exposed to the sunlight. Leaves are also used in a process called transpiration, which helps draw water and dissolved minerals up the plant's stem from the roots, where these substances have been absorbed from the soil. During transpiration, water evaporates through tiny holes in the leaves. More water is drawn up through a thin tube extending down the plant's stem.

Himalayan Balsam

WHAT IS POLLEN?

FACT FILE

Bees are attracted to the shape and scent of a flower. They feed on the nectar in the flower and gather pollen, which they store in sacs on their legs to take back to the hive.

Pollen is the plant's equivalent of an animal's sperm: it carries the male reproductive genes. Pollen consists of tiny grains, each with a tough coat that is often patterned with characteristic ridges and spikes. When inhaled, the fine pollen causes allergies such as hay fever in some susceptible people. Pollen can be found in fossil deposits, making it possible to identify the plants that were living then – even though no actual plant fossils may be found. Pollination takes place when a pollen grain is deposited on the tip of a pistil (part of the female reproductive system of a plant). The grain then grows a long tube down inside the pistil that fuses with the egg cell and completes the process of fertilization.

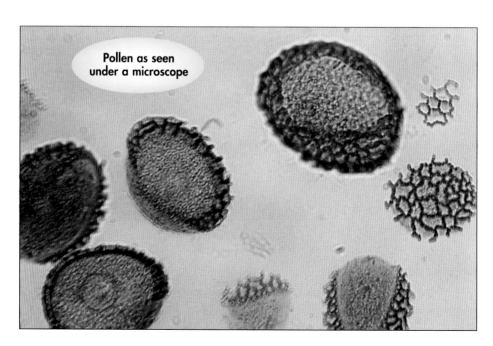

Pollen as seen under a microscope

WHAT ARE LICHENS?

Lichens are peculiar organisms in which algae and fungi live together. They are usually flat and crust-like, with no roots and often grow on roofs, rocks (*below*) or tree branches. Some grow like a small branched tree, while others can be found hanging from tree branches (*right*). The main structure of a lichen is the fungal part, but it also

contains algae cells which contribute food through photosynthesis. Lichens grow very slowly, but can eventually cover very large areas. Some individual ones are extremely old, and some lichens growing in rocks in Antarctica are thought to be 10,000 years old – they are the oldest living organisms.

FACT FILE

Reindeer moss is a form of lichen that is very common throughout the Arctic. It forms the main diet of the caribou and other grazing animals.

Red-banded
web-cap

WHAT ARE FUNGI?

FACT FILE

Fungi have been a popular food for hundreds of years, even as far back as Roman times. A number of species such as the truffle, cep and mushroom are delicious and safe to eat. A great many, however, are not edible.

Fungi used to be considered a part of the plant kingdom, but they are now thought to be quite different. The main part of the fungus is a mass of tiny threads called mycelium. Fungi live on other organic matter. In the soil, fungi are the most important agent in the breakdown of dead plant and animal material, recycling it so that plants can use the nutrients. Fungi live in damp areas or in water because they have no method of preventing their fragile threads from drying out – they cannot survive dry atmospheres. There are around 50,000 species of fungi and they include yeast, rusts, smuts, mildews, moulds and mushrooms.

WHAT ARE ALGAE?

Algae are the most primitive form of plant life. Most algae are aquatic, and they range in size from microscopic single-celled organisms to seaweed that is several feet long. Algae photosynthesize, like other plants, and they are responsible for providing most of the world's oxygen. Algae are very varied, but even the large forms, such as kelp and other seaweeds, lack the true leaves, stems and roots found in other plants. Not all algae use the green chlorophyll found in other plants in order to photosynthesize, some use red or brown pigments for this purpose.

WHAT ARE PERENNIAL PLANTS?

Perennial plants survive from one year to the next. They usually grow quite slowly, and can afford to build up their strength before they need to produce seeds. The parts of perennial plants that are above the ground are generally killed by frost in the autumn, but the roots and/or underground parts live through the winter. Growth is renewed and the cycle begins anew in the spring.

Perennial plants that grow in arid or desert conditions commonly survive dry times by becoming physiologically inactive. In some cases they remain alive but are dehydrated until water becomes available, at which time they rapidly absorb moisture through above-ground parts, swelling and resuming physiological activity. Some plants can absorb dew, which for many is the main water source. Mosses and lichens adopt this strategy, as do some flowering plants, which are sometimes called resurrection plants.

Daffodil

Early purple orchid

FACT FILE

As well as looking very like small bees, the flowers of bee orchids actually produce a female bee 'smell'. They are therefore highly attractive to male bees.

WHAT ARE BONSAI TREES?

Bonsai trees are decorative miniature trees or shrubs. The art originated in China, where, perhaps over 1,000 years ago, trees were cultivated in trays, wooden containers, and earthenware pots and trained in naturalistic shapes. Bonsai, however, has been pursued and developed primarily by the Japanese.

They are dwarfed by a system of pruning roots and branches and training branches by tying them with wire. Some of these trees are very old and are perfect miniatures, even producing tiny flowers or cones.

WHAT ARE NETTLES?

FACT FILE

The nettle family includes a diversity of plant types that range from small herbaceous species to large trees. Among the members are stinging nettles; mulberry, fig and elm trees; hop vines; and hemp.

The nettle family is comprised of about 45 different species of herbs, shrubs, small trees, and a few vines, distributed primarily in tropical regions. Many species, for example the Stinging Nettle (or *Urtica*) have stinging hairs on the stems and leaves. The leaves are varied and the sap is usually watery. The small, greenish flowers often form clusters in the leaf axils. Both male and female flowers may be borne on the same plant. The curled stamens of the male flowers straighten quickly as the flowers open, releasing the pollen. The dry, one-seeded fruit often is enclosed by the outer whorl of the flower cluster. The dead-nettles are so called because many of them have leaves like the stinging nettles, but they have no sting. The main characteristic of this large family are the square stems, opposite leaves and whorls of irregular flowers.

Yellow Archangel

Dandelion

WHAT IS A WEED?

A weed is any plant that grows where people do not want it to grow. A plant may be considered a weed in one place, but not necessarily in another. Some plants such as poison ivy are called weeds wherever they grow because they have no known use. Many weeds are destructive. These species reduce both the quality and quantity of crops by competing with them for sunlight, water, and nourishing substances in the soil. Some types of weeds also shelter insects and diseases that damage nearby crops. Weeds including nettles and poison ivy produce severe skin reactions in most people.

FACT FILE

Weeds can also be beneficial. For example, they reduce the erosion on land where cultivated plants do not grow. They also provide shelter and food for birds and other wildlife. Fireweed, one of many weeds used in making medicines, relieves pain.

WHAT ARE FLOWERS FOR?

FACT FILE

This small elephant hawk moth has visited the flowers of a butterfly orchid during the night for its nectar, and has picked up two yellow pollen masses on its head.

Flowers are the reproductive parts of a plant. Usually one flower has both male and female parts. The male parts are the stamens, which consist of filaments and anthers. Filaments are like little stalks that support the anthers. Anthers produce tiny dust-like grains called pollen. The female part of the flower is called the carpel. This consists of an ovary, ovules, a style and a stigma. The ovary is hidden in a bulb-shaped receptacle at the base of the flower. Inside the ovary are one or more ovules, which become seeds if the flower is fertilized. In order for a flower to be fertilized, pollen must be transferred from the male stamen to the female stigma.

WHAT IS THE TALLEST TREE IN THE WORLD?

The Californian giant redwood is one of the oldest and largest living organisms on Earth. They often exceed 90 m (300 feet) in height, and their trunks reach typical diameters of 3 to 6 m (10 to 20 feet). The redwood tree takes 400 to 500 years to reach maturity, and some trees are known to be more than 1,500 years old. These ancient trees have very few branches and leaves, and are often scarred by fire and lightning strikes. As the tree ages, the lower limbs fall away, leaving a clear, columnar trunk.

FACT FILE

The oldest-known trees are bristlecone pine trees. They grow in the White Mountains in California, in the USA. Although they are quite small, some of these gnarled trees are more than 4,500 years old.

WHAT ARE PLANTS USED FOR?

Over thousands of years, human beings have found many uses for plants. Some of the most common ones are shown here:

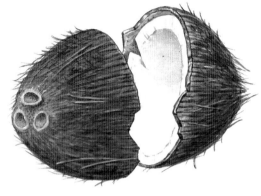

Coconut skins are used for matting. Sisal and hemp are also tough threads used for ropes and matting.

Most paper is made from cellulose found in wood pulp.

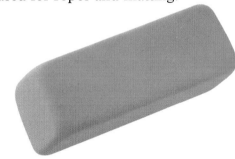

Rubber comes from the sap of a tropical tree and is used for many things including tyres, wellington boots and erasers.

FACT FILE

And of course we eat plants every day of our lives in one form or another.

Many plant extracts are used in the making of medicines.

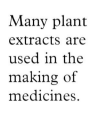

WHAT ARE UMBELS?

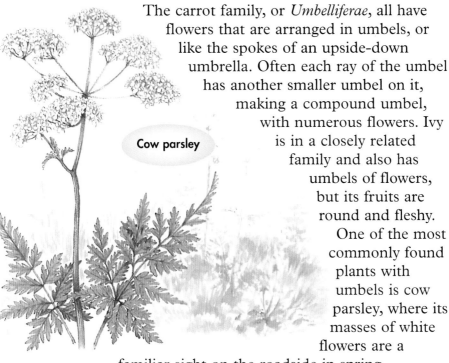

Cow parsley

The carrot family, or *Umbelliferae*, all have flowers that are arranged in umbels, or like the spokes of an upside-down umbrella. Often each ray of the umbel has another smaller umbel on it, making a compound umbel, with numerous flowers. Ivy is in a closely related family and also has umbels of flowers, but its fruits are round and fleshy.

One of the most commonly found plants with umbels is cow parsley, where its masses of white flowers are a familiar sight on the roadside in spring.

FACT FILE

Some of our familiar vegetables, such as parsnip and carrot, have been developed from wild plants of the this family.

Ivy

Clearing ponds to maintain population

WHAT IS CONSERVATION?

Over the last few decades very large areas of natural habitats, once rich in plant and animal life, have disappeared under buildings, roads and farms. Modern farming methods, with large fields, intensive use of pesticides, and high crop yields, do not give many wild flowers and animals a chance to survive. Nowadays, most species survive in places where these changes have not taken place – old woodland and heathland, for example. However, natural habitats are disappearing fast, and constant effort is needed to conserve what is left. Otherwise they may deteriorate so much that they become unsuitable for species that depend on them for survival.

FACT FILE

A few plants are now so rare that they have become valuable. Some collectors or dealers attempt to dig up the rarest plants, such as orchids, so that they can sell them. Conservation organizations may erect special cages or mount 24-hour watches to protect them.

WHAT IS POLLUTION?

Pollution is the name we give to waste products that enter the air, soil and water, but cannot be quickly broken down by natural processes. Instead they affect the health of plants and animals, including humans, and the environments they live in. Controlling the emissions of factories and vehicles can help. It is also important, as far as possible, to use materials that can break down in the soil when they are thrown away.

Such materials are said to be bio-degradable.

One of the saddest sights is that of dead fish floating on the water. One of the most frequent ways they are killed is when the water is polluted by chemicals.

FACT FILE

Rivers and canals are often used as unofficial dumping sites for household waste. To improve matters, there are new laws to protect the environment. But we all need to help to keep the environment clean and healthy.

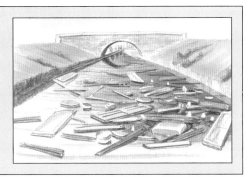

OUTER

SPACE

CONTENTS

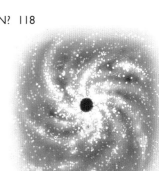

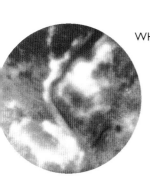

WHAT IS A SPACE SHUTTLE?

A space shuttle is the first re-usable spacecraft. It was developed to provide a re-usable, and therefore cheaper, vehicle for launching satellites and for other work in space. The shuttle is a bulky delta-winged aircraft with powerful rocket motors. At launch, two solid-fuel booster rockets are strapped to its sides, and a giant fuel tank is fixed to its belly. The rockets and fuel tank fall away after launch, and the rockets are recovered and re-used. In orbit, the shuttle's cargo bay opens to release satellites or allow the crew to work in space. The shuttle lands on a runway like a conventional aircraft.

Launching a space shuttle

FACT FILE

At takeoff the space shuttle weighs 2,000 tonnes. It burns almost all of its fuel in the first few minutes after launch, then continues to coast into its orbit 300 km above the surface of the Earth.

WHAT ARE THE BENEFITS OF SPACE EXPLORATION?

Leaving the launch pad

FACT FILE

The Hubble Space telescope was launched in 1990 as a revolutionary piece of equipment for astronomers. Hubble is able to focus on objects not visible to the human eye.

Until 1957, human beings were just observers of the solar system. Now they have entered the realm of space and gathered firsthand knowledge of their planetary environment. Twelve men have landed on the Moon, set up data-gathering experiments on the lunar surface, and brought back lunar rocks and soil for study and analysis. The hidden side of the Moon and the planets Mercury, Venus, Mars, Jupiter, and Saturn have been photographed and studied. The Earth and its weather have been studied, and communication relays and navigational aids have been established.

WHAT IS A SPACE STATION?

Space stations allow the crew to work in space for long periods in conditions of zero gravity. While conditions in space capsules and the space shuttle are cramped, space stations are more suitable for longer stays in space. Rockets or the space shuttle bring supplies of air and food to the space station, and often a replacement crew. Space stations are constructed from modules that are small enough to be carried by rockets or the space shuttle, which are assembled once they are in orbit.

FACT FILE

Skylab was the first US space station. One of its tasks was to test how humans behaved in microgravity.

Space station

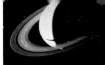

WHAT DO SPACE SATELLITES DO?

Space satellites have revolutionized communications, making possible everyday developments such as mobile phones and television. Communication satellites receive signals beamed at them from the Earth, and send them on to other places. They transmit television and telephone signals around the world, even to remote areas. They are also used for defence communications, including checking on the movement of military forces. Satellites can survey the Earth's surface, predict weather changes and track hurricanes. They can also help to examine resources such as crops, forests and even minerals.

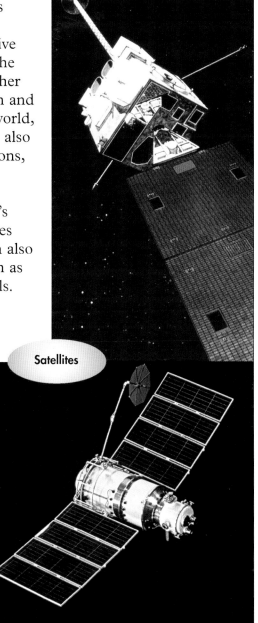

FACT FILE

Navigation satellites enable people on land or at sea to work out their exact map position to within a few feet.

Satellites

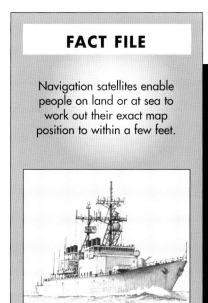

WHAT IS THE MOON?

The Moon is the Earth's only satellite, and it has been orbiting our planet for at least 4,000 million years. It is a rocky sphere about 3,476 km in distance, which is about one-quarter the size of the Earth.

Scientists believe that the Moon formed when another planet about the size of Mars collided with the Earth. The collision splashed a huge mass of molten (liquid) rock into space. This molten rock quickly formed into a sphere, and the Moon rapidly cooled into its solid form. The Moon's surface is heavily pitted by collisions with debris such as asteroids.

FACT FILE

Living things need air and water to stay alive, and neither of these is available on the Moon. The Moon also suffers extreme temperature swings between the lunar day and night.

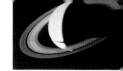

WHAT IS THE MOON MADE OF?

The Moon is a rocky satellite, and is made of similar material to the Earth. It has an outer layer, or mantle, of rock, and a core that is probably made up mostly of iron. Unlike the Earth's liquid mantle, the interior of the Moon is cool and solid. There is little or no volcanic activity on the Moon. However, while it was cooling, early in its life, floods and streams of lava ran out across the Moon's surface. The Moon also has mountain ranges, many of which are the remains of impact craters and volcanoes that were active when the Moon was still hot.

There are some huge valleys called rilles, which can be hundreds of miles in length and look a little like river-beds.

WHAT IS A LUNAR MONTH?

The Moon revolves around its own axis every 29½ days, which is also the time it takes to complete one orbit around the Earth. This period of time is known as a lunar month.

The ancient Egyptians originally employed a calendar based upon the Moon, and, like many peoples throughout the world, they regulated their lunar calendar by means of the guidance of a sidereal calendar. They used the seasonal appearance of the star Sirius; this corresponded closely to the true solar year, being only 12 minutes shorter. Certain difficulties arose, however, because of the differences between lunar and solar years. To solve this problem the Egyptians invented a civil year of 365 days divided into three seasons, each of which consisted of four months, of 30 days each. To complete the year, five extra days were added, so that the 12 months were equal to 360 days plus five extra days. The lunar calendar regulated religious and everyday life.

FACT FILE

The appearance of the Moon alters, depending on the position of the Sun in relation to the Moon. The Sun lights up only one side of the Moon. As the Moon orbits the Earth, we see this lit-up area from different angles.

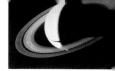

WHAT MAKES THE MOON SHINE?

The Moon is by far the brightest object on the night sky, but it has no light of its own. Moonlight is simply the reflected light of the Sun. Parts of the Moon that are not in sunlight are invisible against the deep blackness of space. Although the Moon appears bright and silvery, only a small proportion of the light that falls on it from the sun is reflected back towards us. This is because the Moon's surface is grey and rocky, and does not reflect light well. When the Sun is off to one side, part of the Moon is in deep shadow and all we can see is a thin slice, or crescent, of the Moon's lit surface. The far side of the Moon was a mystery until 1959, when a Soviet space probe took the first photographs of it. The actual appearance of the far side was something of a disappointment, because it had far fewer craters than the familiar side that always faces Earth.

FACT FILE

A solar eclipse can only happen when the Earth, the Moon and the Sun are all aligned. These eclipses may be total or partial depending on the exact alignment of the three bodies.

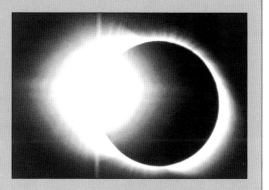

WHAT IS THE EARTH MADE OF?

The Earth is a big ball, or sphere, made mostly of rock. Inside the earth the rock is melted, but the outside cover is hard rock. Less than one-third of the earth's surface is land and more than two-thirds are water.

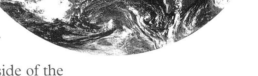

To go into a little more detail, the outside of the Earth is a crust of rock about 10 to 30 miles thick. The high parts of this crust are the continents and the low parts of it hold the waters of the oceans and the great inland seas and lakes.

The crust of the Earth has two layers. The upper layer, which makes the continents, is made of granite. Under the layer of granite is a thick layer of very hard rock called basalt. Scientists believe that at the core of the Earth is a huge ball of molten iron, with a diameter of around 4,000 miles.

FACT FILE

The Earth is thought to be about 4,600 million years old. The oldest rocks so far discovered are up to 3,800 years old. We can calculate the age of the Earth by examining meteorites, and changes in atomic structure.

WHAT IS THE WEIGHT OF THE ATMOSPHERE?

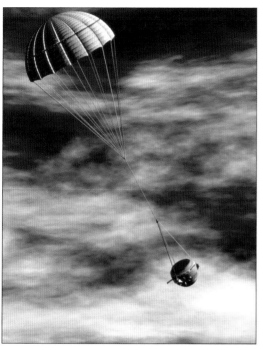

The Earth is surrounded by a thick blanket of air. This is its atmosphere. The Earth's atmosphere is made up of about 20 different gases. The two main ones are oxygen and nitrogen. It also contains water and dust particles. Air is matter, and like all matter it has weight. Weight is the measure of the pull of gravity on matter. If a scale registers ten pounds when a stone is placed on it, this means that gravity is pulling the stone with a force of ten pounds. Similarly, Earth's gravity pulls on each particle of gas and dust in the atmosphere. Because our atmosphere is a vast ocean of air, it has considerable weight. If it could somehow be compressed and put on a set of scales, it would weight about 5,700,000,000,000,000 (5,700 quadrillion) tons! The Earth's atmosphere is one of the things that makes it a planet of life.

FACT FILE

Our knowledge of air pressure has enabled us to understand the physics behind aircraft flight. Air passing over the top of a plane's wings reduces in pressure, allowing higher pressure under the wings to exert an upward force, so the plane can fly.

WHAT MAKES THE EARTH TRAVEL AROUND THE SUN?

According to one theory about the origin of the solar system, about 5 billion years ago, a huge dust cloud was formed and began to spin.

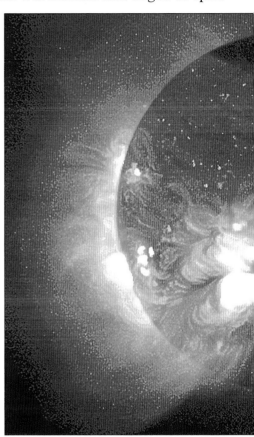

It flattened into a disk, and the hot central mass became the Sun. The outer parts of the dust cloud broke away in swirling masses, and became the planets. So why didn't these planets just fly off into space? The answer is gravitation, or the pull of the Sun. This outside force keeps the Earth in motion around the Sun.

A planet moves in its orbit at a speed that depends on its distance from the sun. The planet moves faster when it is closer to the Sun than when it is farther away. The Earth moves at a speed of 18.8 miles per second when it is closest to the Sun, and 18.2 miles per second when its orbit takes it farthest from the Sun.

FACT FILE

Other planets that revolve around the Sun are Mercury and Pluto. Mercury is the closest planet to the Sun and moves at an average speed of 29.8 miles per second.

WHAT IS THE SUN MADE OF?

The Sun is a great ball of hot gases, made up of many layers. Astronomers have obtained many of their facts about the Sun by

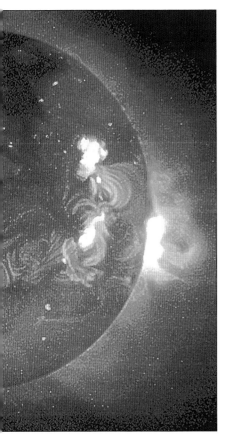

using special instruments. These instruments enable the scientists to study the glowing gases of the Sun and to see how different substances are distributed on the Sun and to take photographs of the Sun's corona without causing damage to the eyes. Finally, these instruments study radio waves that are emitted by the Sun. Because the Earth's atmosphere stops many of the Sun's radiations from reaching the Earth, scientists send

instruments high up into the atmosphere. Such space probes help them learn more about the Sun.

FACT FILE

Without the sun, life would be impossible on Earth. Among other things, the atmosphere would be frozen, no green plants would be living, and there would be no rain.

WHAT KEEPS THE SUN SHINING?

FACT FILE

As stars go, our Sun is very small. It is of a type known as a yellow dwarf. The colour of a star shows its surface temperature: red stars are relatively cool, while blue stars are hotter.

Our Sun is a star and, like in most other stars, a process called nuclear fusion is taking place at its core: atoms of hydrogen collide and are combined into atoms of helium at very high temperatures and pressures. In the formation of the helium atoms tiny amounts of mass are lost and converted into a huge amount of energy.

Over millions of years, this energy makes its way out from the core of the Sun and eventually reaches the Sun's surface where it is emitted as light, heat, ultraviolet radiation and X-rays. From the surface of the Sun, it takes about eight minutes for the light and other radiation to reach the Earth.

Fusion started in the Sun about five billion years ago and, although 600 billion kilograms of hydrogen is being converted to helium every second, it will continue to do so for about the same length of time.

WHAT ARE SUN SPOTS?

FACT FILE

The Aurora Borealis (in the north) and the Aurora Australis (in the south) happen as charged particles cascade through the Earth's magntic field. One massive solar flare in 1989 caused a power cut in Canada that left 6 million people without electricity.

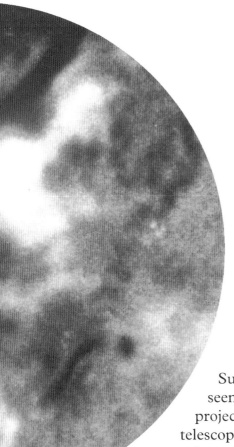

Sunspots are darker areas that can be seen on the surface of the Sun if projected onto a piece of card through a telescope. They appear dark because they are about 2000°C cooler than the area around them, but they are still about 4000°C. They are caused by regions of the Sun's visible surface becoming trapped in twisted areas of magnetic fields. The numbers of sunspots varies over an eleven-year cycle.

Sunspots are associated with other events on the sun, such as solar flares, when vast amounts of high-energy particles are ejected from the Sun. If these head towards the Earth, they can effect radio and television signals, and can cause auroras as they bump into the Earth's magnetic field. When a flare is detected on the Sun, astronauts in the International Space Station head for one chamber, which is better protected from solar radiation than the rest.

WHAT IS THE MILKY WAY?

FACT FILE

There are at least 3,000,000,000 stars in the galaxy. And here is an idea of its size. It takes eight minutes for light from the Sun to reach the Earth. For light from the middle of the galaxy to reach the Sun, it takes about 27,000 years.

There is probably nothing more mysterious and wonderful-looking in the sky than the Milky Way, stretching like a band of jewels from one end of the sky to the other. In early Christian times people thought it was a pathway for the angels, so they could go up to heaven on it. But today we know the real facts about the Milky Way. Our galaxy is shaped roughly like a watch, round and flat. If you could get above it and look down on it, it would look like an immense watchface. But we are inside the galaxy, and when we look up we are looking towards the edge from inside the 'watch'. So we see that edge curving around us. As there are millions of stars in it, we see it as the Milky Way.

WHAT IS A STAR?

Stars are huge balls of burning gas that are scattered throughout the Universe. They burn for millions of years, giving off both light and heat. Stars produce energy by a process called nuclear fusion. The coolest stars are red and dim, while the hottest stars give off blue-white light. The temperatures on their surface range from 3,500°C for cooler stars to over 40,000°C for the hottest stars.

A new star is born when gas and dust are drawn together by gravity, forming a huge clump. It heats up until nuclear fusion begins, and the new star appears in the sky.

FACT FILE

Stars die when they eventually use up all their fuel and burn out, but this process takes many millions of years. Towards the end of its life, a star starts to run out of hydrogen to power its nuclear fusion. It starts to cool, becoming a red giant.

WHAT KEEPS THE STARS SHINING?

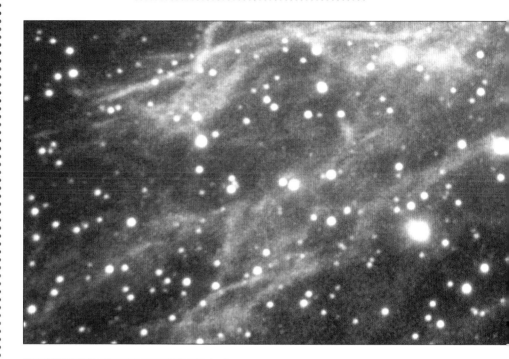

FACT FILE

The farthest stars in our galaxy are 80,000 light-years away. The nearest star to the Earth is our own Sun, which is 152 million km away.

Just like the Sun, a star is a ball of very hot gas which shines by its own light. If you look up at the stars in the night sky perhaps you have noticed that they seem to twinkle. This is caused by substances in the air between the star and the Earth. The unsteady air bends the light from the star, and then it seems to twinkle.

It is now believed that hydrogen atoms in the very core of the star burn to form helium. When this happens, it sets free energy which flows steadily to its surface. Stars should be able to continue radiating this energy for many millions of years to come.

WHAT ARE SHOOTING STARS?

Shooting stars, or meteors, are streaks of light that cross the night sky, although they can only be seen for one or two seconds. They are caused when a solid piece of rock called a meteoroid plunges through the Earth's atmosphere, burning up due to air friction. If, as rarely happens, a small fragment reaches the Earth, it is called a meteorite. Sometimes these fragments of rock move through space as a meteor swarm or stream. They move in regular paths, and the larger fragments become detached and travel individually.

FACT FILE

This impact crater in Arizona was caused by a huge meteorite. The amount of energy the impact released would have been equivalent to hundreds of nuclear weapons.

WHAT IS A SUPERNOVA?

Sometimes a star appears in the sky quite suddenly. This happens when there are a pair of stars rotating together. These are called binaries, and there is usually one large star called a red giant, orbiting with a smaller, hotter star. The nova takes place when gas is drawn from the red giant into the smaller star, where the heat causes a massive explosion and emits huge amounts of light. A supernova takes place when a star collapses as it begins to burn

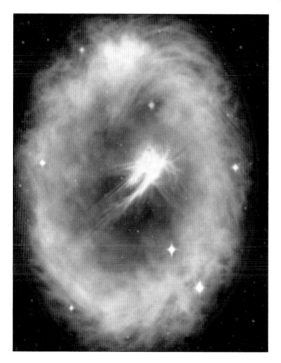

out, then suddenly explodes, producing a huge amount of light energy, and leaving behind a tiny core of neutrons, which is the heaviest substance in the Universe.

FACT FILE

Even with today's most powerful and advanced equipment, there is no visible limit to the Universe. No one is totally sure of the shape of the Universe.

WHAT IS A NEBULA?

FACT FILE

The only diffuse nebula visible to the naked eye is the beautiful Orion Nebula.

A nebula is a huge cloud of white-hot gas and solid material that whirls about in interstellar space getting smaller and hotter all the time. As the gas cloud gets smaller, it throws off rings of gas. Each of these rings condenses to become a star. Based on appearance, nebulae can be divided into two broad classes: dark nebulae and bright nebulae. Dark nebulae appear as irregularly shaped black patches in the sky and blot out the light of the stars lying beyond them. Bright nebulae appear as faintly luminous, glowing surfaces; they either emit their own light or reflect the light of nearby stars.

127

WHAT ARE THE PLANETS OF THE SOLAR SYSTEM?

The four planets that are nearest to the Sun are called the inner planets. In order from the Sun, they are Mercury, Venus, Earth and Mars. The inner planets are different from the outer planets, which are farther away from the Sun, because they are made of rock. Each of the inner planets has an atmosphere. However, apart from the Earth, the atmospheres of the inner planets are very thin and would be poisonous to humans. The outer planets, which are Jupiter, Saturn, Uranus, and Neptune (Pluto was downgraded to a dwarf planet in 2009) are composed mainly of frozen gases, and are large but light.

FACT FILE

Science fiction writers thought that life might exist beneath the thick clouds of Venus. We now know that conditions there are too extreme for life as we know it.

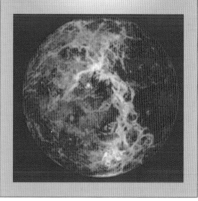

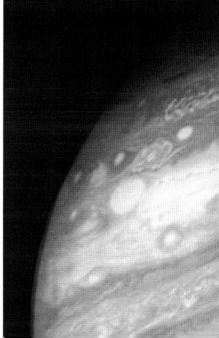

WHAT ARE THE RINGS OF SATURN?

FACT FILE

Pluto is now considered a dwarf rather than a true planet. It is on the edge of deep space. It was only discovered in 1930, as a result of calculations to find out why Neptune's orbit was being disturbed by an unknown body.

Shining rings of billions of tiny chips of ice, rock and dust surround Saturn. The rings reflect light strongly and can be clearly seen through a telescope from the Earth. It was first thought that Saturn had three wide rings, but it is now known that the rings are actually made up of thousands of narrow ringlets. The rings are only 100 m (328 ft) thick, but they extend into space for 76,000 km (47 mi). The material in the rings was probably captured by Saturn's gravity when the Solar System was forming, or it might be the remains of a moon that has broken up. Recently, space probes discovered that some of the rings are braided, or twisted.

WHAT MAKES NEPTUNE BLUE?

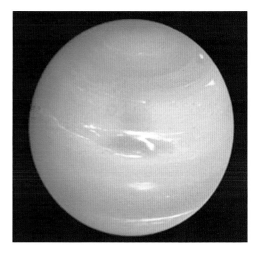

Neptune is covered with a blue ocean of liquid methane. It is a very cold place – at the farthest part of its orbit it is 4,000 million km from the Sun. Its surface temperature drops to –210°C. Neptune is made of hydrogen, helium, and methane, and probably has a rocky core. It takes an amazing 164.8 years to travel just once around the Sun. Neptune was first identified in 1846 when astronomers found that an unidentified planet was disturbing the orbit of Uranus. Neptune has huge storms and one of these, the Great Dark Spot, was larger than the Earth.

FACT FILE

Mars is covered by a stony desert that contains lots of iron oxide, making it appear rusty-red. Mars has small polar ice-caps that grow larger during the Martian winter.

WHAT IS A PLANETARY SATELLITE?

A satellite is a natural or artificial object that revolves around a larger astronomical object, usually a planet. The Moon is the most obvious example. All the planets in the solar system except Mercury and Venus have natural satellites. More than 60 such objects have so far been discovered. Saturn has the most satellites, with 18 certain and several more yet to be confirmed. The natural satellites vary greatly in size. Some of them measure only several km in diameter, as in the case of the two tiny moons of Mars and the outer satellites of Jupiter.

FACT FILE

Ganymede is the largest satellite of Jupiter. It was discovered by the Italian astronomer Galileo Galilei in 1610 and named by the German astronomer Simon Marius after a figure in Greek mythology.

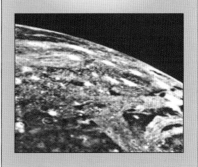

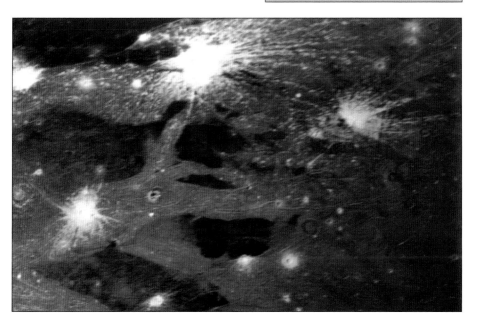

WHAT ARE MOONS?

A moon is any natural satellite orbiting a planet. All the planets in our Universe have moons with the exception of Mercury and Venus. Earth only has one moon and that is the Moon itself, which takes a total of 27.3 days to orbit our planet. Pluto also only has one called Charon which takes 6.4 days to orbit. Next comes Mars which has two moons called Phobos (0.3 days to orbit) and Deimos (1.4 days to orbit). Neptune has eight moons which take anything from 0.3 days to 360.2 days to orbit. Uranus has 15 moons with orbiting times of between 0.3 and 13.5 days. Next is Jupiter with 16 moons with orbiting times of between 0.3 and 758 days to orbit. Finally Saturn has 18 moons with orbiting times of 0.57 to 550.4 days.

Titan

Ganymede

FACT FILE

Io is one of the moons that orbits Jupiter. Its diameter is 3,640 km, it is 421,800 km from Jupiter and takes a total of 0.7 Earth days to orbit the planet.

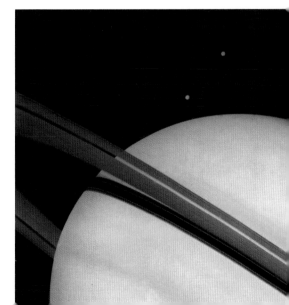

WHAT ARE PLUMES?

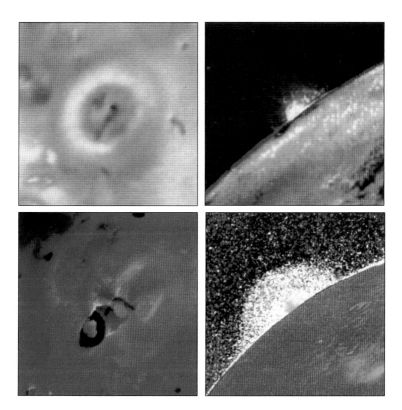

Originally it was thought that inter-planetary space was empty of matter except for that thrown out from the Sun, and for the clouds of particles that became visible as meteoroids on striking the Earth's atmosphere at night. From space exploration it has been learned that the solar wind flows continuously and at such velocities (from 400 to 500 km per second) that the particles escape the solar system. These are called plumes.

Earlier it was believed that the existence of electric fields in space was unlikely. Evidence based on measurements in space indicates that such fields do exist.

FACT FILE

A spiral galaxy is one with a central hub from which emerge spiral arms. Spiral galaxies are usually made up of old and young stars, and large amounts of dust.

WHAT DOES VENUS LOOK LIKE?

Venus is often referred to as Earth's sister. The planet is a similar size to our own, but here the resemblance ends. The temperature on the surface of the planet is nearly 500°C (930°F). The air is dense enough to crush a human in seconds, and the atmosphere consists partly of acid. The dark patches that you see on the surface of Venus are a layer of cloud 30 km (19 miles) thick. If we look past the clouds, we can see that Venus is a planet once ruled by volcanoes. There are at least 160 that are larger than 100 km (62 miles) in diameter and over 50,000 smaller ones. However, there is no evidence to show that these volcanoes are still active today.

FACT FILE

Because Venus was the Roman goddess of love, astronomers have named many of the planet's features after famous women.

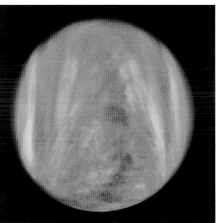

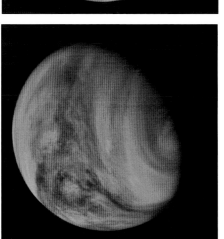

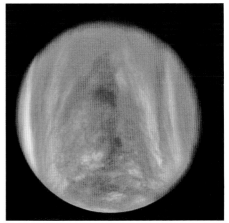

WHAT DOES THE EARTH LOOK LIKE FROM SPACE?

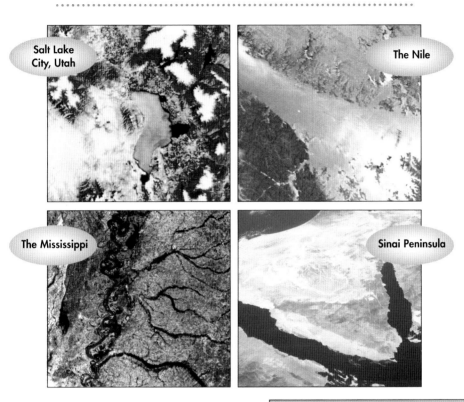

Salt Lake City, Utah

The Nile

The Mississippi

Sinai Peninsula

Earth is designated in astronomy as the third planet outward from the Sun. Its single most outstanding feature is that its near-surface environments are the only places in the universe known to maintain life. Those who have gone into space have come back with a changed perspective and reverence for the planet Earth. The effect from space is obvious. One astronaut said after his trip, "My first view – a panorama of brilliant deep blue ocean, shot with shades of green and grey and white – was of atolls and clouds."

FACT FILE

Pioneer 10 was the first man-made object to leave the Solar System. It carried messages about life on Earth to be read by any extraterrestrial travellers who might find the probe.

WHAT IS THE TAIL OF A COMET?

You cannot see the nucleus (centre) of a comet with the naked eye but you can sometimes see its tail. It appears as a smear of light that very gradually moves across the sky. As a comet moves closer to the Sun, the ice and other frozen gases in its nucleus begin to boil off, producing a long tail of gas and dust. The tail will always point away from the Sun because light and other forms of radiation from the Sun push against the minute particles that are present within the tail.

Comet tails are very different in shape and size. Some are short and stubby. Others are long and slender. As the tail grows, the comet gains in speed because it is nearing the sun.

A comet showing its tail

FACT FILE

Halley's Comet is perhaps the most famous comet of all. It can be seen from Earth every 76 years and was even recorded in 1066 on the Bayeux Tapestry.

WHAT IS A BLACK HOLE?

Black holes are the monsters of the Universe. Formed from the brightest of all explosions, supernovae, they soon become the darkest objects in space, emitting no light at all.

A black hole is an area in space where the force of gravity is so strong that even light cannot escape from it. Black holes are created when a burned-out star collapses. Eventually it shrinks into a tiny sphere of material. The gravity of this material is so powerful that it pulls in everything around it. Even light itself

is sucked into the black hole. Nothing that goes into a black hole ever comes out. Although we cannot see black holes, we can sometimes identify them from the radio waves given off as a star is drawn into one.

FACT FILE

Imagine space as a stretched-out sheet. If an object is placed on this sheet, it will create a dip, towards which other objects will be drawn if they come too close. A black hole creates such a steep dip that objects that enter can never escape.

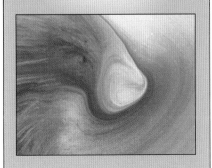

TELL ME WHAT : OUTER SPACE

WHAT WAS THE BIG BANG?

Nobody knows how the Universe began, but the most common theory is the Big Bang. According to this theory, the Universe was formed from an immense explosion 13 billion years ago. Before the Big Bang, everything in the Universe was packed into a tiny area, smaller than the nucleus of an atom. This point was called a singularity and was incredibly hot. It was released in an explosion so powerful that all of the matter in the singularity was blasted into an area larger than a galaxy in less than a fraction of a second. There is very strong evidence to support the theory of the Big Bang. The strongest 'proof' is a weak signal that has been detected in space. This is thought to be an echo from the energy released by the force of the Big Bang.

FACT FILE

According to ancient Egyptian mythology, the essentials of life – air (Shu) and moisture (Tefnut) – came from the spittle of their Sun God Re. From the union of Shu and Tefnut came Geb, the Earth god, and Nut, the sky goddess. The first human beings were born from Re's tears.

WHAT IS THE UNIVERSE MADE UP OF?

The Universe is everything and anything that exists. The Universe is still a mystery to scientists. The Universe is made up almost entirely of hydrogen and helium. These are the two lightest elements. All the rest of the matter in the Universe is very rare. Elements such as silicon, carbon and others are concentrated into clouds, stars and planets. The Universe is held together by four invisible forces. Gravity and electromagnetism are the two familiar forces. The other two kinds are strong and weak nuclear forces. These operate only inside the incredibly tiny nuclei of atoms, holding the tiny particles together.

FACT FILE

The large Hadron Collider, successfully tested in 2010 will teach us more about particle acceleration and the birth of stars and the deepest laws of nature.

HISTORY

AND EVENTS

CONTENTS

. . . .

WHAT IS STONE HENGE?

Stone Henge on Salisbury Plain

More than 5,000 years ago Europeans were building spectacular stone monuments. Many of these are still standing today, as mysterious relics of a long-gone society. The huge stones that were used are called megaliths (meaning 'big stones'). Some were set up on their own, and others in groups or circles.

Stone Henge is a very famous Neolithic stone monument which was built in several stages between 1800 and 1400 BCE on Salisbury Plain. No one really knows why it was built. It is a series of concentric rings of standing stones around an altar stone at the centre. During the second stage, blue stones from the Preseli Mountains in Wales were hauled onto the site in an astonishing feat of organization and transport. The construction was highly accurate for the period. The standing stones are up to 6.7 m (22 ft) high and weigh up to 40 tonnes (45 tons) each.

FACT FILE

Rock tombs, slab tombs, such as this dolmen, and stone circles and temples lie scattered across Europe, even on the island of Malta.

WHAT ARE HIEROGLYPHICS?

Egyptian picture-writing is known as hieroglyphics. This language is made up of about 750 signs, with pictures of people, animals and objects. Until hieroglyphics was deciphered in modern times, it was not known that most of the pictures represented sounds and syllables, not whole words. Scribes used a quick form of writing which was called hieratic. The Egyptians were also good at maths, particularly geometry, which they used in architecture and surveying. They drew up an accurate 12-month calendar of 365 days, and used water clocks to measure time.

Chest from tomb of Tutankhamun

FACT FILE

The Egyptian Sun god Re was often portrayed in picture form simply as a sun disk. He appeared in other forms too, including a cat, bird and a lion.

WHAT WERE THE FIRST RULING DYNASTIES IN CHINA?

From a hazy mixture of history and legend, we learn that China's first ruling family was the Hsia. The legendary first emperors are said to have tamed the rivers, so that farmers could grow millet and wheat. The first rulers known from archeological evidence were the Shang. From about 1500 BCE, they controlled the best farmland – around the Huang He valley – and from here their power spread.

The Shang kings were cruel, ruling in barbaric splendour. They built China's first cities, and were expert at making cooking pots, tools and weapons. Shang rule lasted until 1122 BCE. By then the rulers had become tyrants.

FACT FILE

An example of Chinese writing on silk. The Chinese wrote in picture signs, and made up about 50,000 characters. The first important work of Chinese literature dates from before 1000 BCE.

The Shang kings were superstitious. They consulted 'oracle bones' before making any important decision. A soothsayer would read the signs in animal bones cracked by heat, and advise the king accordingly.

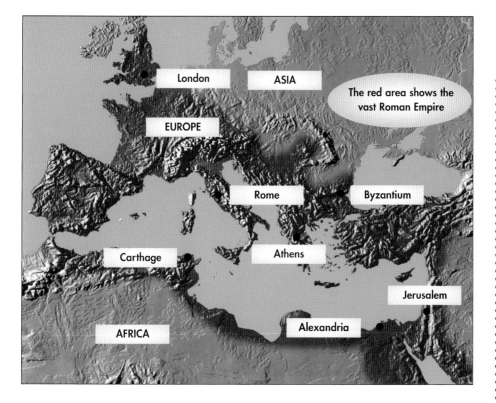

London   ASIA

The red area shows the vast Roman Empire

EUROPE

Rome   Byzantium

Carthage   Athens

Jerusalem

AFRICA   Alexandria

WHAT WAS THE EXTENT OF THE ROMAN EMPIRE?

FACT FILE

Slaves made up about a third of Rome's population. At the slave auctions, slaves wore tags advertising their skills and good character.

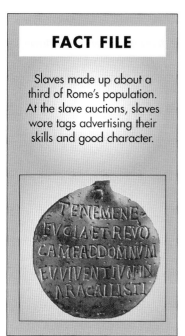

Rome grew from a small kingdom in Italy. It became a republic and one of the mightiest empires of the ancient world, with an empire stretching the length of the Mediterranean Sea.

At its peak, the Roman Empire stretched from Britain in the west to Mesopotamia in the east. The army defended this empire well. Rome rose to power thanks to its fertile farmland, its army and its key position in the middle of Italy. As well as fighting, Roman soldiers built roads, forts and aqueducts. Most people accepted Roman rule without question, because of the benefits it brought, letting them farm and trade in peace.

WHAT WAS THE BYZANTINE EMPIRE?

The Roman Empire split in two in CE 395. After the collapse of the western half in CE 476, the eastern part survived. Its capital was called Byzantium (now Istanbul in Turkey), a city founded by the Greeks. The Roman emperor Constantine gave the city of Byzantium a new name, Constantinople.

The Byzantine Empire swallowed up Turkey, the Balkans, parts of Spain and North Africa, Egypt and the western coasts of the Mediterranean. The Empire was at its height under the rule of the 19th-century emperor Justinian and his influential wife Theodora. Through war and diplomacy, Justinian made Byzantium the greatest power in the eastern Mediterranean.

FACT FILE

Byzantine traders used gold coins called bezants. These coins have been found across Asia as far as China and as far west as the British Isles.

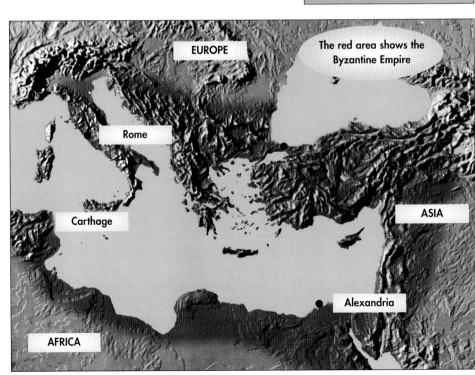

The red area shows the Byzantine Empire

EUROPE

Rome

Carthage

ASIA

Alexandria

AFRICA

WHAT WAS EARLY MONASTIC LIFE LIKE?

In the CE 500s, an Italian named Benedict of Nursia drew up a set of rules for monks (or people in monasteries). All monks must be poor, unmarried and obedient. Monks wore simple robes, shaved their heads, and shared all their daily tasks.

Monasteries were for men only. Religious women joined orders of their own and became nuns. Each monastery was led by an abbot, some of whom had as much power as any nobleman, controlling farms, trades and even private armies.

Monks grew their own food, reared farm animals, baked bread and brewed beer. They made their own clothes and furniture, and built their own churches. They also looked after the sick. Part of their time was spent teaching young boys, who would in time become monks themselves.

FACT FILE

The monastery at Mont Saint-Michel in France was built by Benedictine monks in CE 966. It stands on a tiny island in Normandy, linked by a causeway to the French mainland.

WHAT IS SUTTON HOO?

The most powerful ruler among the English kings was acknowledged as 'Bretwalda', or supreme king.

The Sutton Hoo ship burial site in Suffolk was discovered in CE 1939. It is almost certainly the monument to King Redwald of East Anglia, who was Bretwalda in the CE 620s, and who died in CE 627.

Artefacts unearthed by archaeologists at the Sutton Hoo site included a gold belt, a sword and a shield. There were also several items of jewellery. Most importantly there was a sceptre and standard which must have belonged to the dead King Redwald. The iron helmet (*right*) was another one of the treasures to be unearthed at Sutton Hoo.

FACT FILE

The Scots' leader Kenneth MacAlpin, was the first king to rule the land we now call Scotland. Raiders from the north, Picts and Scots, attacked northern England once the Roman army were no longer around to protect the Roman Britons of England.

WHAT WERE THE CRUSADES?

The Byzantine emperor, a Christian monarch who lived in Constantinople, needed help. He turned to the pope, who in 1095 called for all Christians to start a holy war against the Suljuk Turks.

Thousands rushed to join the Crusader armies. They crossed into Palestine and recaptured the important cities of Nicaea and Antioch. Jerusalem fell in 1099 after a desperate siege lasting six weeks, and the Crusaders took terrible revenge by slaughtering thousands of Muslims. There were to be three more crusades: one in 1144, the second in 1187 and finally the Children's Crusade in 1212. Fifty thousand children set off from France and Germany for the Holy Land. Many died on the journey, many more were captured and sold as slaves in Africa.

FACT FILE

Richard I of England and Philip II of France led the armies of the Third Crusade, setting sail for the Holy Land in 1189.

WHAT WAS THE MAGNA CARTA?

The youngest son of Henry II, John, inherited from his brother Richard the throne of England, as well as the Plantagenet dominions of France, which he had lost to the French by 1204. John's failure to recapture these territories, his dispute with Rome over the Pope's choice of a new Archbishop of Canterbury, and a high level of taxation, had the English nobility up in arms against him.

Magna Carta

In 1215 they forced the King to agree to the Magna Carta, guaranteeing their rights in relation to those of the crown. It was intended to protect the rights of nobles, and made sure that no-one was imprisoned without a fair trial. Copies of this document, which tried to put an end to the king's abuse of his power, were distributed across the whole of England. This led to civil war, which only ended with John's death in 1216.

Despite all these disasters, it is now known that John was a much better king than history has actually portrayed him.

John

FACT FILE

The magnificent coronation of Charles V. He became king of Spain in 1516 (he was the grandson of King Ferdinand and Queen Isabella of Spain), and three years later he was crowned Holy Roman Emperor.

WHAT WAS THE BLACK DEATH?

The bubonic plague (or 'Black Death') was a disease which brought death to most parts of Asia, North Africa and Europe. The first outbreak was recorded in 1331 in China. The plague started as a bloody swelling in the armpit or groin and quickly invaded the whole body. It was highly contagious and killed millions of people. The infection probably began on the steppes, the grassy plains of Asia. It was carried by fleas which lived in the fur of the black rat. The rats lived close to humans and thus the disease spread rapidly. Corpses were left out in the road for people to collect, thus causing the disease to spread even further.

FACT FILE

Medieval paintings often depicted death as a skeleton, dancing and leading victims to their end. The epidemic killed at least 25 million people in Europe and the Near East.

WHAT DO WE KNOW ABOUT THE EARLY HISTORY OF AFRICA?

We know very little about the early history of Africa. There must have been great civilizations there, but very few of them developed writing or left any records. Some civilizations built fine communities, such as the east coast port of Kilwa or the mysterious stone complex of Great Zimbabwe. After about CE 700, Muslims from the Near East began to take over many coastal regions and trade routes.

FACT FILE

A view showing what the Great Enclosure inside the city of Great Zimbabwe may have looked like.

One of the wealthiest of the medieval African empires was Mali. Starting in 1240, its Islamic rulers built up a kingdom stretching for around 1,600 km over West Africa. Much of the land was desert, but Mali grew rich from gold.

The Great Mosque of Djenné in Mali

152

By 1550, Spain ruled most of Central and South America and the West Indies. Fleets of Spanish galleons carried gold, silver and plundered treasures across the Atlantic to Europe.

WHAT WAS THE NEW WORLD?

FACT FILE

A modern replica of the Mayflower, the ship in which the first Pilgrims set sail from England in 1620.

From 1492 onwards, European explorers sailed across the Atlantic to what they called the New World of North, Central and South America. There they discovered a treasure trove of gold and silver. They also found foods that only grew in the New World, such as sweetcorn, potatoes and plants that could be made into medicines.

The people that settled in the New World were traders rather than soldiers. Their first contact with the people already living there was friendly. The Native Americans showed the newcomers how to hunt, fish and farm in a land of plenty. In return they were given objects such as knives, needles, fish hooks and cloth.

WHAT WAS THE INDUSTRIAL REVOLUTION?

One of the biggest changes in the history of the world, the Industrial Revolution, started in Britain in the late 18th century. As the 'Workshop of the World' Britain was the first home of new machines, new types of materials and new ways of making power. This was the age of coal and iron, of gas and electricity, of railways and factories.

These factories created millions of new jobs, so many people began to leave the countryside to work in the towns. Houses and factories had to be built for them. By 1850, over 60 per cent of Britons lived in towns. Factory workers led hard lives, often working 14 hours a day, six days a week.

FACT FILE

Raw cotton, grown mainly in the USA, was very difficult and slow to clean. Whitney's cotton gin was a simple machine which brushed out the seeds from the cotton.

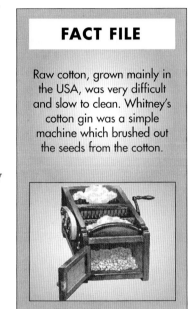

Ironworks at Coalbrookdale in Shropshire

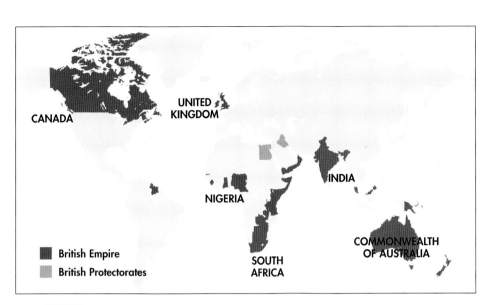

British Empire

British Protectorates

CANADA

UNITED KINGDOM

NIGERIA

INDIA

SOUTH AFRICA

COMMONWEALTH OF AUSTRALIA

WHAT WAS THE EXTENT OF BRITAIN'S COLONIES IN THE 18TH CENTURY?

Britain had started her collection of overseas colonies in the reign of Elizabeth I. By 1602, both England and the Netherlands had founded an 'East India Company' on the Indian coast to trade with the Far East.

The first settlements in North America took root and flourished in early Stuart times. In 1661, Britain gained her first African foothold, seizing James Island on the Gambia River. By the middle of the 1700s, these scattered colonies had begun to grow into a powerful and profitable empire. By the 1750s the British navy ruled the waves. By 1763 Britain had won most of France's territory in North America. The map above shows the extent of the empire in 1821.

FACT FILE

British General James Wolfe brought French power in North America to an end. Wolfe's troops attacked and seized the town of Quebec. He died before the battle of Quebec ended.

WHAT WAS THE MEIJI RULE?

The 1860s was a time of uncertainty and political unrest in Japan. Finally, in 1868, the situation became so serious that Emperor Mutsuhito took control from the last shogun (military dictator). Mutsuhito became known as the Meiji emperor, and this event is called the 'Meiji restoration'.

Under the emperor's authority, Japan embarked on a programme of modernization. In 1872, a group of Japanese politicians went on a tour of Europe and North America to learn more about industry, education and ways of life in the West. As a result, factories were built in Japan and the country started to change from an agricultural to an industrialized nation. This also included the establishment of a national railway system. During the period of Meiji rule, education was introduced for all Japanese people. The Meiji emperor also gave farmers ownership of their lands and changed Japan's army and navy into modern military forces.

FACT FILE

During the Meiji period, Japan wanted to extend its territories. In 1894–5 its forces crushed the Chinese navy and gained control of Taiwan. Here you can see a Chinese ship sinking during the battle of Yalu in 1894.

WHAT WAS HOME RULE?

In 1870, a movement calling for Home Rule was founded in Ireland. Supporters of Home Rule wanted a separate parliament to deal with Irish affairs in Dublin. Although the British government was forced to introduce many reforms, two bills to introduce Home Rule were defeated in parliament in the 1880s and 1890s. William Gladstone was Prime Minister of Britain four times during the reign of Queen Victoria. He believed that the Irish should run their own affairs and was a staunch supporter of Home Rule. But he failed to get his Home Rule Bill approved by parliament. During World War I, the issue of Home Rule continued to cause conflict in Ireland. The third Home Rule Bill had been passed by the British parliament in 1914, but the outbreak of war in the same year delayed the start. Irish protestants, however, were bitterly opposed to Home Rule. They were in the majority in the northern province of Ulster, and believed that they would be treated unfairly by a Dublin parliament. They formed the Ulster Volunteer Force to protect themselves if Home Rule was introduced.

William Gladstone

FACT FILE

Irish politician Charles Parnell addresses an audience in support of Home Rule. He became leader of the Home Rule Party in the British parliament and fought tirelessly for his beliefs.

The Suez Canal

WHAT IS THE SUEZ CANAL?

The idea of a canal linking the Mediterranean to the Red Sea dates back to ancient times. It was Napoleon's engineers who, around 1800 CE, revived the idea of a shorter route to India via the Suez Canal. It was not until 1859 that Egyptian workers started working on the construction of the Canal in conditions, described by historians, as slave labour. The project was completed around 1867.

Although Britain had played no part in building the Suez Canal in Egypt, it benefited greatly when it opened. The new 190 km (118 mi) waterway shortened the route from Britain to India by around 9,700 km, thereby extending their powers of trading.

FACT FILE

Queen Victoria was on the throne when the Suez Canal was first started and when it opened. During her reign, which lasted 63 years, Britain's empire expanded greatly.

WHAT WAS 'CUSTER'S LAST STAND'?

The Battle at Little Big Horn

George Armstrong Custer first came to prominence as a cavalry officer during the American Civil War (1861–1865). In 1866 he led the 7th Cavalry against the Native Americans of the Great Plains, and in 1874 he led an expedition that discovered gold in the Black Hills of the Dakota Territory and started a gold rush. The hills were sacred to the Cheyenne and Sioux Indians and relations between these people and the white invaders deteriorated. In 1876, Custer led the 7th Cavalry against an alliance of Cheyenne and Sioux warriors. He went into battle against thousands of warriors in the valley of the Little Big Horn River. He and his main unit of 250 soldiers were all killed in what became known as 'Custer's Last Stand'.

FACT FILE

Bold pioneers made their way in long trains of covered wagons, drawn by the stories of gold in the hills. However, very few actually made their fortunes.

WHAT WAS STEPHENSON'S ROCKET?

FACT FILE

In 1840, the American Inventor Samuel F. B. Morse launched a code based on dots, dashes and spaces. Known as the Morse code, it speeded up the sending of messages through the telegraph.

Modern rail travel owes its existence to the great engineer George Stephenson. While working as a mechanic in a coal mine, he educated himself at night school. By 1812, he was a chief mechanic and, in 1814, he built his first locomotive, the *Blucher*. This locomotive propelled itself at 6 km (4 miles) per hour and could pull eight wagons loaded with coal. Stephenson refined the steam engine until, in 1829, he built the first practical steam locomotive, the *Rocket*. It could travel at an amazing 58 km (36 miles) per hour.

George Stephenson

WHAT WAS THE WOMEN'S MOVEMENT?

The women's movement had its roots in the late 1700s and early 1800s. Changes such as the American and French revolutions promoted ideas of 'equality' and 'liberty', yet women were not permitted to vote, and most had limited access to education.

In 1792, a British writer called Mary Wollstonecraft published *A Vindication of the Rights of Women*, setting out her belief in equal rights for men and women. This idea took a firm hold during the 1800s, and many women started to campaign for reform. The suffragettes engaged in many different forms of protest, including chaining themselves to railings outside the residence of the British Prime Minister.

FACT FILE

In Britain, the suffragette campaigners often went on hunger strike when imprisoned for their actions. The authorities did not want them to die, and arouse public sympathy, so they fed the women by force.

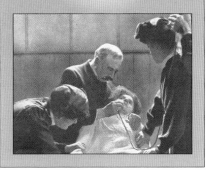

WHAT WERE THE SLUM CITIES OF 19TH CENTURY BRITAIN LIKE?

The events of the Industrial Revolution brought great changes to towns and cities in Britain. People needed to live close to their work-place, so huge numbers of houses were put up to accommodate this new class of industrial worker. The speed with which many towns and cities expanded led to problems with overcrowding, dirty and insanitary housing. Many workers were forced to live in slum conditions. Worse, the new factories created pollution that often contaminated both water supplies and the air. Early industrial cities were disease-ridden places with very high death rates.

FACT FILE

Life in the industrial centres revolved around the mines, mills and factories where people worked.

Pollution from the new factories

WHAT WAS THE GREAT DEPRESSION?

A disastrous stock market crash in 1929 in the USA left many people penniless overnight. The effects of the Wall Street Crash were felt all over the world. Many countries in Europe were hard hit because they had borrowed money from the USA at the end of World War I. Throughout the 1930s, unemployment soared and trade slumped in a period known as the Great Depression.

During the worst years of the Depression, many people were forced to rely on charity and government hand-outs for their most basic needs. In 1932 Franklin D. Roosevelt was elected US present. His 'New Deal' aimed to create jobs and to protect people's savings by regulating banks more closely.

FACT FILE

This is the Stock Exchange in Wall Street at the time of its collapse. You can see brokers spilling out onto the streets of the city of New York.

The Lusitania

WHAT WAS THE GREAT WAR?

Before the war, Germany had built up its navy to match the strength of the British navy. From the start of the Great War, the name by which World War I was first known, British warships blockaded German ports. In this way Britain's navy prevented supplies from reaching Germany, causing severe shortages of food and other goods.
The Germans retaliated with their submarines, called U-boats. After 1915, U-boats attacked both warships and merchant shipping carrying supplies to Britain. In May 1915, a German torpedo hit a British passenger ship called the *Lusitania*. The ship was carrying nearly 2,000 passengers, including many Americans.

FACT FILE

The battle of the Somme took place in northern France in 1916. It lasted for around five months, during which time over one million soldiers were killed.

WHAT WAS THE TREATY OF VERSAILLES?

The signing of the Treaty of Versailles

FACT FILE

The signing of the Treaty of Versailles on June 28, 1919, in Paris was the fifth anniversary of the shooting of Archduke Ferdinand in Sarajevo.

The Treaty of Versailles was a peace document signed at the end of World War I by the Allied and Associated Powers and by Germany. It took place in the Hall of Mirrors in the Palace of Versailles, France, on June 28, 1919 and actually came into force on January 10, 1920.

The treaty was drafted during the Paris Peace Conference in the spring of 1919, which was dominated by the national leaders known as the 'Big Four', David Lloyd George of Britain, Georges Clemenceau of France, Woodrow Wilson of the United States and Vittorio Orlando of Italy. They wanted to make sure that Germany would never again pose a military threat. The treaty contained a number of stipulations to guarantee this aim.

WHAT WAS THE EASTER RISING?

During World War I, the issue of Home Rule continued to cause conflict in Ireland. When war actually broke out in 1914, most Irish Volunteers supported Britain in its fight against the Central Powers. But a breakaway group formed the Irish Republican Brotherhood (later known as the IRA). On Easter Monday, 1916, protesters belonging to this and other nationalist movements seized buildings in Dublin and proclaimed Ireland a republic. This rebellion became known as the Easter Rising.

FACT FILE

The British Prime Minister, David Lloyd George proposed that Ireland would stay under British control, but the Irish Free State would become a British dominion.

Easter Monday, 1916

WHAT WAS THE BATTLE OF BRITAIN?

FACT FILE

Allied troops wait on a beach at Dunkerque, in northern France, in June 1940. A rescue fleet of naval ships, fishing boats, yachts and ferries sailed across the English Channel from England to carry them back to safety. In all, 300,000 soldiers were rescued.

During World War II the Allied forces of Britain and France became trapped by the rapid German invasion. In June 1940, the French signed a truce with Germany and Britain stood alone against the Germans.

Italy joined the war, siding with the Germans. In June 1940 Hitler made plans to invade Britain. However, he first needed to gain control of the skies. The Battle of Britain began in July 1940 between the German airforce, the Luftwaffe, and Britain's Royal Air Force (RAF). By May 1941 the RAF had gained the upper hand and Hitler stopped bombing Britain.

WHAT WAS THE HOLOCAUST?

Jews held in a concentration camp

In the early 1930s, the Nazi party rose to power in Germany, led by Adolf Hitler. He set up a secret police force, banned opposing political parties and started to persecute minority groups in the German population, such as gypsies and Jews.

During World War II concentration camps such as Belsen and Auschwitz were set up by the Nazis. Millions of Jews were imprisoned and murdered in these camps because Hitler believed they were responsible for the downfall of Germany. An estimated six million Jews died in these camps in World War II, an event known as the Holocaust.

FACT FILE

The official flag of the United Nations consists of a map of the world circled by two olive branches. The olive branches are a symbol of peace.

WHAT WAS THE BLITZKRIEG?

FACT FILE

World War II had deadly new weaponry as well. The introduction of machine guns changed the way that they fought from the trenches. They could now easily wipe out large numbers of attacking soldiers.

World War II was very different to the first international conflict. Trench warfare, which had claimed so many lives, was now an outdated concept. When Adolf Hitler invaded Poland in September 1939, he unleashed a new and frightening brand of warfare into the world – called 'Blitzkrieg' or lightning war.

The key to the success of Blitzkrieg was the use of tanks in very large numbers and innovative style. The tanks charged ahead independent of the troops and wreaked havoc among defenders. Bursting through defensive lines they created confusion and smashed supply lines.

Tanks used during Blitzkrieg

WHAT IS COMMUNISM?

Communism is a system of political and economic organization in which property is owned by the state and all citizens share the common wealth, more or less according to their needs.

After years of civil war, much of China was in ruins. Mao Zedong set about reforming the country according to communist ideals. Land was seized from landowners and divided up among the peasants. In Mao's 'Five-Year Plan' (1953–1957) new roads and railways were built, industry boosted, and health and education improved. Mao printed his ideals about his communist state in what became known as Mao's 'Little Red Book' which was read by millions of Chinese.

FACT FILE

Chairman Mao and his supporters accused many people of failing to follow communist ideals. Students and young people formed groups of 'Red Guards' in support of Mao.

WHAT IS THE UNITED NATIONS?

At the end of World War I in 1918, many people were determined that there should never again be such terrible slaughter and bloodshed. An international association called the League of Nations was formed by the leading nations involved in the war. Peace and security are the most important aims of the United Nations. Since 1945, the UN has helped to negotiate peace deals and has provided peacekeeping forces. In addition to working for peace, the UN has many other branches, called agencies, that deal with worldwide problems. Some of these agencies provide aid for people in need, such as refugees. Others are concerned with health matters, living and working conditions, and human rights.

Representatives from 26 countries

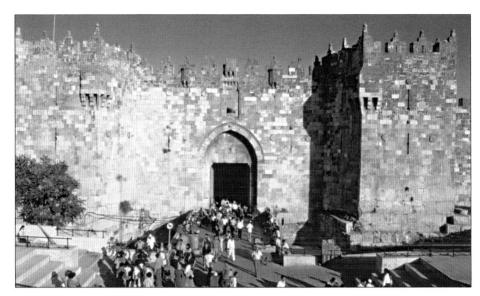

WHAT IS ZIONISM?

By the early 20th century, Jewish people lived all over the world, particularly in European countries, the USA and Russia. In the late 1800s, some Jews had established a movement known as Zionism.

The Zionists called for Jews to return to the area around Jerusalem, which they considered their spiritual homeland. Part of the Turkish (Ottoman) Empire was inhabited largely by Arabs. As more and more Jews arrived in the area of Palestine, tension grew between the Arab inhabitants and Jewish immigrants. In 1917, the British government issued the Balfour Declaration, offering support for a Jewish homeland in Palestine. Jewish immigration increased rapidly in the 1930s as thousands of Jews fled Nazi persecution.

FACT FILE

Israel has borders with Lebanon and Syria, Jordon and Egypt. In 1967 Israel occupied the territories of the Gaza Strip and the West Bank, home to over one million Palestinian Arabs, and the Sinai Peninsula.

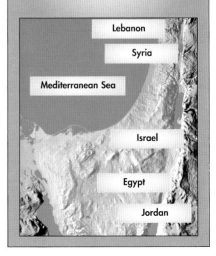

Lebanon

Syria

Mediterranean Sea

Israel

Egypt

Jordan

WHAT WAS THE CUBAN MISSILE CRISIS?

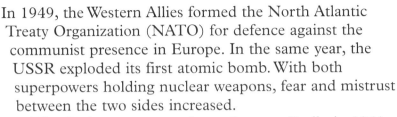

In 1949, the Western Allies formed the North Atlantic Treaty Organization (NATO) for defence against the communist presence in Europe. In the same year, the USSR exploded its first atomic bomb. With both superpowers holding nuclear weapons, fear and mistrust between the two sides increased.

The Soviets constructed a wall across Berlin in 1961, separating East from West in the city. In 1962, the Cuban crisis erupted when the USA discovered that the USSR was building missile sites on the island of Cuba in the Caribbean. These sites were within range to launch an attack by nuclear weapons on American cities. The two superpowers came to the brink of war before the USSR agreed to withdraw the weapons.

Although the two superpowers never became involved in direct warfare, both sides became involved in wars elsewhere in the world. The USA fought communism and the USSR helped communist fighters.

The Vietnam War between North and South Vietnam lasted from 1957 until 1976. This is a statue of remembrance in Washington D.C.

FACT FILE

John Fitzgerald Kennedy was US president from 1961 until he was assassinated in 1963. During his presidency the Berlin Wall was built, dividing the city in two and stopping East Germans escaping communist rule.

GENERAL

KNOWLEDGE

CONTENTS

· ·

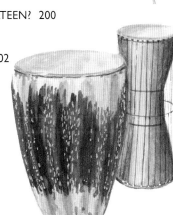

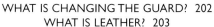

WHAT IS SAND MADE OF?

Erosion constantly wears away solid rock through the action of rain, snow and waves, frost and ice, glaciers and wind and the bits broken off are slowly broken down into ever-smaller pieces.

The most common mineral found in sand is quartz but other minerals, such as calcite, feldspar and mica are also present.

The colour of sand on a beach reflects the material from which it is made: in Hawaii sands from volcanic rocks are black while those of coral islands are very pale because they are formed from the ground-down skeletons of long-dead coral polyps rather than from eroded rock.

FACT FILE

Sand is a very useful substance. It is used in making concrete, in making glass, in sandpaper and as a filter in helping keep water pure. And of course children love to play in sand with a bucket and spade.

WHAT IS A SCORPION?

Scorpions are distant relatives of spiders, but while spiders bite, scorpions carry their venom in poison glands near the stinger that they carry at the tip of the tail.

Many scorpions live in arid areas, such as deserts, where they will shelter from the heat of the day under stones or in the burrow of another animal, and hunt insects at night. Other species live in jungles and shelter under bark during the day.

When a scorpion spots prey, it raises its tail ready to strike, and once it has caught its victim

Scorpion

paralyses or kills it by stinging it.

A scorpion will also raise its tail as a display when it meets anything that it sees as a threat, such as a meerkat or a large spider.

Scorpions range in size from those that are only 1 or 2 cm as full-grown adults to as much as 17 cm. None will deliberately attack a human, except in self-defence so people may get stung if they accidentally disturb one.

FACT FILE

There is a fly called a scorpion fly which has the characteristic scorpion tail. The long beak-shaped mouth is suited to scavenging for meals.

WHAT WERE THE FIRST CLOCKS LIKE?

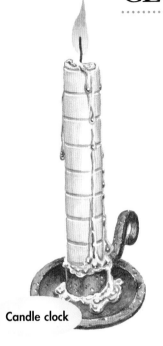

Candle clock

The sundial was one of the earliest devices for measuring time. But it can work only on a day with plenty of sunlight. Early peoples also used ropes with knots tied at regular intervals. In the ninth century candles were marked with regularly spaced lines, but this was not very accurate as a draught could cause the candle to burn more quickly. When burned, such devices measured time. An hourglass or sandglass tells time by means of sand trickling through a narrow opening. A water clock, or *clepsydra*, measures time by allowing water to drip slowly from one marked container into another. By the 1700s, people had developed clocks and watches that told time to the minute. Modern electronic and atomic clocks can measure time with far greater accuracy.

Sundial

FACT FILE

The Sun was man's first clock. Long ago men guessed at the time of day by watching the Sun as it moved across the sky. It was easy to recognize sunrise and sunset, but harder to know when it was noon, the time when the sun is highest above the horizon.

WHAT COUNTRY PRODUCES THE MOST CLOCKS?

If we think about different types of clocks and watches, we associate some of them with different countries: grandfather clocks and marine chronometers from England, cuckoo clocks from both Germany and Switzerland, precision-engineered jewelled watches from Switzerland, too, and digital watches from countries in south-east Asia such as Japan. Watches are very important to the Swiss economy as these expensive items are sold all over the world.

Of course, many of the other items that we have in our homes also have clocks in: video-recorders, DVD-players, PCs, microwave ovens and cameras all tell the time. As most of these goods are made in south-east Asia, we can safely say that most clocks are made there.

Grandfather clock

Wristwatch

Digital alarm clock

FACT FILE

The first mechanical alarm clock was invented in 1787 by a Mr Hutchins of New Hampshire, and the first wind-up alarm clock that could be set for any time was devised by a Mr Thomas in 1876.

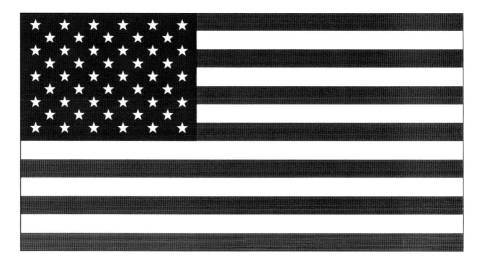

WHAT IS THE
'STARS AND STRIPES'?

Stars and Stripes – also called 'Old Glory', or 'Star-spangled Banner', is the flag of the United States of America. It consists of white stars (50 from July 4, 1960) on a blue background, with a field of 13 alternate stripes, 7 red and 6 white.

The 50 stars stand for the 50 states of the Union, and the 13 stripes stand for the original 13 states that signed the Declaration of Independence.

After the beginning of the American Revolution, the first unofficial national flag – known variously as the Grand Union Flag, the Great Union Flag, or the Cambridge Flag – was hoisted outside Boston, on January 1, 1776. It was hoisted, it appears, at the behest of General George Washington, whose headquarters were nearby. The flag had seven red and six white horizontal stripes and, in the background, the British Union Flag (the immediate predecessor of the Union Jack).

FACT FILE

In 1775 George Washington was elected as commander-in-chief of the colonists' army. He became a leading symbol for independence.

WHAT MAKES A BASEBALL CURVE?

Baseball

The ability to make a ball swerve through the air rather than follow a straight line is a valuable one in many sports, whether as a pitcher in baseball, a spin bowler in cricket or a footballer taking a penalty. The curve occurs because of the 'Bernoulli effect', which was discovered by scientist Daniel Bernoulli.

Basketball

When the player wants to make the ball follow a curve through the air, he makes it spin as it leaves his hand or foot. As it spins, air is pulled with it through friction, and this works together with the current created by its motion through the air. On one side of the ball, the air passing it and the air spinning around it go in the same direction, allowing it to move faster, while on the other side of the ball, the air spinning around it is in the opposite direction to the air current passing the ball, which slows it down and makes it curve.

Rugby ball

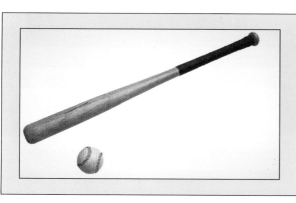

FACT FILE

In 1989, Bill White became the first Afro-American to head a major U.S. sports league when he was named president of baseball's National League.

WHAT WAS THE FIRST MUSICAL INSTRUMENT?

Panpipes

According to an ancient Greek myth, the god Pan invented the first musical instrument – the pipes that are named after him – after he accidentally breathed heavily through old reeds beside a river and produced a wail. He so liked the sound that he broke the reeds off and tied them together. Because the reeds were different lengths they produced different notes. Although this is a myth, not reality, it shows that most early musical instruments may have been made because someone noticed a natural effect and decided to make use of it. The first instruments were probably drums, made of hollow logs, and sticks that were hit together to provide a beat for dancing. Animal horns were later used to make simple wind instruments and early stringed instruments include the lyre, in which strings are strung from a simple frame and plucked.

FACT FILE

The valves on brass instruments allow players to play different notes by changing the length used. This means that the player can use just one mouthpiece.

African drums

WHAT IS JAZZ?

Jazz is a form of music that originated in the southern United States in the late 19th century, as a development of the songs and spirituals of Afro-American slaves, with melodies that incorporate both African and European music. It is a strongly rhythmic form of music, incorporating elements of ragtime, the blues and folk music. One popular early form came from New Orleans and was sometimes called Dixieland jazz, which could be deeply emotional. In improvized (or improv.) jazz, the players make the music up as they go along. Jazz is also renowned for long soloes by players such as clarinettists and saxophonists. Jazz led

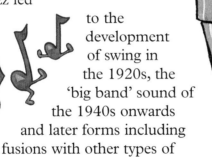

to the development of swing in the 1920s, the 'big band' sound of the 1940s onwards and later forms including fusions with other types of music, such as funk, and free jazz.

FACT FILE

The 'blues', which was an important factor in jazz, was also instrumental in the development of many other major forms of popular music including rock'n'roll, as in many of Elvis Presley's songs like 'Heartbreak Hotel', and country and western.

Man-made pearls

WHAT IS A CULTURED PEARL?

Pearls, whether natural or cultured, are made in the bodies of some species of oysters and are composed of the same material as the irridescent mother of pearl that lines oysters' shells, which is a form of calcium carbonate. If something, such as a grain of sand, gets into an oyster's shell, it will not be able to expel it and instead coats it with layers of mother of pearl, creating a spherical pearl. Because natural pearls are rare, people make cultured ones by inserting a grain of sand into oysters in order to force them to create pearls, which are harvested after two or three years. These are usually lower in quality than natural pearls and often not perfectly spherical. Because of this, and because they are less rare than natural pearls, cultured ones are less expensive to buy.

FACT FILE

Because oysters in the wild can live for a long time, pearls can grow to enormous sizes as the animal adds layers of mother of pearl for year after year.

WHAT DOES AN OCTOPUS EAT?

FACT FILE

The Portuguese man-of-war is one of the largest jellyfish. Its tentacles contain a very dangerous toxin, which can be fatal to humans in large doses. It can grow up to 20 m (66 ft)

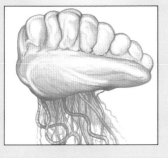

There are more than 150 species of octopus, ranging from the very small to the giant octopus, which may reach 10 m (33ft) in length. Most of them eat crabs, fish, crustaceans and smaller molluscs, which they catch and tear apart with their suckered tentacles. An octopus' mouth is shaped like a parrot's beak, with two very strong jaws. In addition the octopus can inject venom or poison with its bite, which enables it to disable prey that might fight back, such as crabs, more quickly.

Octopus are very intelligent, curious animals, with a highly developed nervous system and extremely good eyesight. They propel themselves through the ocean by squirting water from the edge of their mantle. They are oportunistic feeders, which means that they will tackle almost anything when they are hungry!

An octopus

WHAT IS THE METRIC SYSTEM?

The most widely used system of weights and measures is the metric system, which was devised by a committee of French scientists in 1791. Measures of length include centimetres (cm), metres (m) and kilometres (km); among those for volume are millilitre (ml), centilitre (cl) and litre (l) and for weight milligrams (mg), grams (g), kilograms (kg) and tonnes. Area is measured in metres squared (m^2) and hectares (ha) and temperatures in degrees centigrade (°C), in which water freezes at 0 °C and boils at 100 °C. The measurements are all interlinked: under the correct conditions of temperature and pressure, 1 litre of water weighs 1 kilogram and 1 millilitre (also sometimes called a cubic centimetre) weighs 1 milligram.

Harry weighs 20 stone or 127 kilograms

Susie is running at 4 miles o 6.44 km per hour

FACT FILE

TEMPERATURE

°C	0	20	40	60	80	100
°F	32	68	104	140	176	212

SPEEDS

kmh	20	30	40	50	60	70
mph	13	19	25	31	37	43

WEIGHT

kg	10	20	30	40	50	60
stones	2.8	5.5	8.3	11	13.7	16.5

LENGTH

m	1	2	3	4	5
feet	3.3	6.6	9.8	13.1	16.4

This is 10 ounces of sugar or 283.50 grams

WHAT WAS THE FIRST MEANS OF TRANSPORT?

FACT FILE

Over thousands of years since it was first invented, the wheel has been developed to become more durable, stronger, lighter and more comfortable.

Early man had to rely on his own muscle-power to carry objects, but over thousands of years tamed animals, such as horses, oxen and donkeys, elephants and camels. In order to be able to transport more goods than an animal could carry on its back, sledges and hurdles that could be pulled behind the animal were eventually invented, as well as such intruments as ploughs to make agriculture easier. Where sledges were not suitable, such as on rough ground or sand, he could roll heavy objects along on top of logs, continually taken from behind the object as it passed and placed in front of it. It is thought that stones for both the pyramids and Stonehenge may have been moved using this technique. Eventually, someone realized that attaching the logs, or sections of log, to the object would be more efficient and the wheel was born.

WHAT MAKES PEOPLE LAUGH?

If this question had a simple answer, such as a formula that could be learned, you can be sure that every comedian would know it! But laughter is a complicated thing, and the best explanations of it are still only theories.

We know, of course, that laughter is an expression of many feelings and that laughter is only found among human beings. It is difficult to decide what really makes people laugh, because each person will find a different thing funny. It is all down to being individuals. From the physical point of view, laughter is very good for us. It is good for our lungs, and it is an outlet for some extra energy. So although no one really knows what makes people laugh, or what the purpose of laughter is, it is a very good medicine and certainly makes us feel better.

FACT FILE

When we smile we use 17 different muscles. When we frown we use 43 different muscles. So you can see it is much easier to smile and laugh than to frown and be miserable. Also did you know that your tongue is the strongest muscle in your body!

WHAT MAKES PEOPLE DREAM?

We all dream at night, although we may not remember our dreams in the morning. Although scientists do not precisely understand how we dream, they have discovered that it is important for us to do so and people who are prevented from dreaming soon begin to feel unhappy. We are deeply asleep when we dream, but our brains are active. Scientists think that our brains may be working though the events of the day, storing memories, making sense of our emotions and preparing us for the next day. Dreams are often unrealistic or even weird, putting us in odd situations. Bad dreams, called nightmares, may be particularly vivid and we may be more likely to remember flashes from them because the emotions they created were so strong that they made us wake up.

WHAT IS AN OPTICAL ILLUSION?

The simplest way to describe an optical illusion is that it is a 'trick' that our eyes play on us. We seem to see something that isn't really so. Or we may be able to see the same object in two completely different ways. If our eyes are working properly, and they are instructions for seeing exactly what is before us, how can they play such tricks on us? This is because vision is not a physical process. It is not like photography, for instance, which works mechanically. Vision is really a psychological experience, because it is not the eyes that see, but our brain.

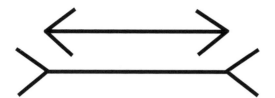

WHICH LINE IS THE LONGEST?

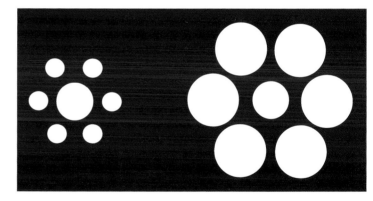

IS THE LEFT MIDDLE CIRCLE BIGGER?

FACT FILE

Our minds love to play tricks on us. We see things in the light of experience. Unless our mind can use the clues it has learned to interpret what we see, we can become very confused. How many legs has this elephant got?

WHAT CAUSES THE LEANING TOWER OF PISA TO LEAN?

Construction of the famous white marble bell tower (campanile) of Pisa's cathedral began in 1173 but by the time three stories were built, it had already begun to lean. Over the centuries, many methods have been tried to prevent the lean getting worse but as most people did not understand what was causing the lean, they made it worse. The soil under the tower is very soft and waterlogged in parts, which is the most plausible explanation for the lean. In 1990, the tower was closed to the public because cracks in the walls were worsening and it was feared that it might topple over. Since then, straps and cables have been used to hold it in place, 800 tonnes of lead weights have been added to the high side of the base and 38 cubic metres of soil removed from that area, which has stablilized the tower, and even reduced the lean slightly.

FACT FILE

It is incredible to think that buildings which were built many hundreds of years ago are still standing today. Castles in particular are a good example of this. Although some may have just their outer walls remaining, it demonstrates just how strong their structure is.

WHAT BIRDS CAN TALK BEST?

Several families of birds can be trained to 'talk', but in reality they are simply mimicking noises without really understanding what they are saying, although they can be taught to associate a given word or phrase with a given action, for example saying 'give us a peanut' to get a reward. The best talkers are parrots and mynas, and members of the crow family such as crows, jackdaws and ravens can also learn a few simple words. They can do this because they are highly intelligent birds and they are excellent mimics in the wild. Other bird mimics that do not pick up speech are starlings and some of the bowerbirds in Australia, including one individual that had learned to copy the noise of the logging machines that were destroying his habitat.

Scarlet macaw

FACT FILE

Many parrots are in danger of extinction, largely because people have destroyed much of their habitat. Some dealers sell illegally captured wild parrots at high prices, risking large fines or even imprisonment.

WHAT HAPPENED TO THE DINOSAURS?

Dinosaurs lived for an enormously long time – some 150 million years – before they died out about 64 million years ago. All the dinosaurs disappeared at about the same time. However, whether this happened over a few days, a few years, one or two centuries, or even a few thousand years is impossible to say.

Many people believe that the dinosaurs became extinct as a result of climate change after a huge meteor or a small asteroid struck the Earth. The extinction of the dinosaurs was not an isolated event. At the same time most marine reptiles and pterosaurs also died out.

Pteranodon

Diatryma

Dimetrodon

WHAT KEEPS A DUCK AFLOAT?

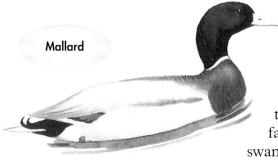

Mallard

It would be easy to think that a duck's feathers would soon become waterlogged so that it would sink, but in fact, ducks, geese and swans, as well as seabirds,

have waterproof feathers, which enable them to swim and dive beneath the surface of the water. Ducks create this waterproofing using the oil from the preen gland, near the base of the tail, which they spread through their feathers and the underlying dense layer of down with their bills. A layer of fat under their breast skin also helps to keep them buoyant. Different ducks feed in different ways, some dive, some upend and feed from the bottom of the lake or river while others 'dabble', stirring up the water with their feet to find food.

FACT FILE

There are about 160 different types of species of ducks in the world, and they are found on every continent except Antarctica. The duck in the picture is called a Pochard.

Red-breasted Merganser

WHAT IS A CLOUD?

A cloud is made up mainly of water. When hot air rises from the land or the sea, it carries water vapour with it. Because the

atmosphere usually gets colder with height, and cold air can hold less vapour than warm air, the vapour eventually condenses in the form of water droplets or ice crystals around particles of dust to form a cloud. If it continues to cool further, the cloud will become denser until the atmosphere is no longer able to hold the moisture and rain, hail or snow will fall. The general rule is that the deeper a cloud is relative to the height of its base above the sea or ground, the more heavily it will rain, hail or snow, so thin, high clouds produce no rain, while thunder storms produce a great deal.

WHAT MAKES STAMPS VALUABLE?

There are a few factors that govern how valuable a stamp is to stamp collectors: the most important is how rare it is. Obviously, very old stamps are uncommon so these, such as the 'Penny Black' very seldom come up for sale and so are unbelievably expensive. Other things that might make a stamp rare might be where a mistake was made in the printing and the stamp was withdrawn after only a few had been sold. Undamaged stamps are more valuable than similar ones that have been damaged.

FACT FILE

In many countries, sets of stamps are issued to commemorate events, such as the 200th anniversary of a person's birth. In the UK, only members of the royal family or entire groups, such as sports teams, may appear on stamps.

WHAT IS GLUE?

Traditionally, glue is made from boiling up the bones, skins and other parts of animals such as fish or horses in order to extract the gelatin, which is then purified and concentrated to make a sticky substance that will form a bond as it dries. There are now many different types of glues, made from plant material or minerals such as petrol, as well as different kinds of synthetic glues. One of the simplest glues is flour-and-water paste and traditional wallpaper paste is made with starch. Latex adhesives were originally made from the latex extracted from rubber trees, but synthetic forms are now also available. Another type of synthetic glue is epoxy resin, in which the user mixes an adhesive substance with equal quantities of a hardener. The two substances react chemically together, causing the adhesive to set rapidly. Glues are widely used in many industries, such as furniture-making and food-packaging.

FACT FILE

In order to protect it and make it last longer, paper money, such as dollar bills or ten-pound notes, is sized with glue. If this were not done, the ink would be rubbed off and the notes would quickly get very dirty.

WHAT MAKES A BOOMERANG RETURN?

The word boomerang is the name given by a particular tribe of native Australians from New South Wales to their traditional throwing stick. There are two forms of boomerang, the curved one that a skilled thrower can get to come back and the nearly straight non-return version. The heavier, straight version is used for hunting, but the curved one is used only for hunting birds and as a way to demonstrate skill. Similar throwing sticks have been used in northeastern Africa, India and Arizona. The returning boomerang is decorated on its top side, which is rounded in the middle and left plain and flat on the bottom. When it is thrown correctly, increased air pressure on the rounded upper surface, in comparison with the flat under surface, causes the boomerang to change direction and return to the thrower. The decorations on boomerangs are often symbolic and relate to native Australian mythology.

FACT FILE

A yo-yo is a child's toy with a string coiled around its middle. If the yo-yo is thrown from the palm of the hand it will sink into a spin at the end of its string before returning back to the hand.

WHAT ARE THE ROMANCE LANGUAGES?

The Romance languages are: Catalan, French, Italian, Provencal, Portuguese, the Rhaeto-Romantic dialects, Romanian, Sardinian and Spanish. They are all descended from Vulgar Latin, which is the term used to describe the version of Latin spoken by commoners in the Roman Empire, instead of formal Classical Latin. In the Roman Empire, locals had to speak Latin, and over time pronunciation and use of words evolved differently in different areas, and other words were taken in from nearby cultures. Although modern English does have a lot of words derived from French, which were absorbed after the Norman Conquest, it is a west Germanic language with Anglo-Saxon roots, as well as elements of the languages of the Vikings.

FACT FILE

Traditionally, love is celebrated on February 14. This is known as Saint Valentine's Day. People often send tokens of affection to their loved ones.

WHAT IS UNLUCKY ABOUT THE NUMBER 13?

13   **13**   13

13   13

13   **13**   13

The answer is that there is nothing unlucky about the number 13, but it is a very widespread and ancient superstition. There are various explanations, including there having been 13 people at the Last Supper or that ancient man could only count to 12 (for which there is no proof). Friday the 13th, is a particularly notorious example of this superstition. Experiments have been conducted to see whether this date is statistically more unlucky than other dates, but have come to the conclusion that it is not and that people are simply more likely to notice when things go wrong on Friday the 13th because of the superstition, whereas they would not think of this a day earlier or a day or week later.

FACT FILE

Other events or items are considered to be unlucky. Some people never open an umbrella up indoors as this may bring misfortune. Others never walk under a ladder, or cross someone else walking up or down a flight of stairs.

WHAT IS A LEPRECHAUN?

Leprechauns (or the little people as some superstitious people prefer to call them) are the mythological fairy cobblers of Ireland. Very difficult to spot, they were thought to look like little old men and hoard treasure. Anyone who managed to catch one could ask for a wish to be granted but they were quite mischievous, so the results might not always be what the person expected. Many cultures have myths of small people, such as Scottish brownies, Cornish piskies (pixies) and a variety of sprites, goblins, elves, gnomes, dwarves and fairies, some of which, like the brownie, were very helpful and others, like pixies and elves, could be very naughty.

WHAT IS CHANGING THE GUARD?

Changing the Guard is a ceremony where the soldiers who have mounted the Queen's guard at Buckingham Palace (the 'old guard') are relieved by the new guard. The responsibility of guarding the Sovereign by the Household Troops (as they were known at the time) dates back to the time of Henry VII (1485-1509).

At Buckingham Palace, the ceremony takes place on alternate days at 11.30am and lasts forty minutes. It takes place inside the palace railings, and it is possible to watch it from outside. The Queen's Guard, accompanied by a band, leaves Wellington Barracks and marches via Birdcage Walk to the Palace.

FACT FILE

Guardsmen such as this one have been wearing bearskin hats since the British defeated the French at the Battle of Waterloo in 1815. The hats have traditionally been made from the fur of Canadian bears, but since these bears are an endangered species, the 'bearskin' hats are now made of fake fur.

WHAT IS LEATHER?

FACT FILE

Among the animals whose skin is used for leather are calves, pigs, horses, sheep, goats, deer, ostriches, alligators, crocodiles, lizards, snakes, seals, whales, sharks, and walruses.

Leather is made of cured animal skin with the hair removed. The first use that man would have made of animal skins was to wrap himself in uncured skins to keep off the cold and wet, but he learned that hanging them in the smoke near a fire prevented them from rotting. Eventually, he discovered that soaking them in water with the bark, leaves or galls of certain trees had the same effect and also softened the hides, making it easier to shape them and remove the hair, as well as changing their colour. The substance that preserves the hides is tannin, and the process is called tanning. Modern synthetic chemicals are also now used, as well as chemical dyes that can give the leather bright colours.

WHAT IS CAMOUFLAGE?

In the natural world, many animals are coloured so that they blend in with the habitat in which they live: polar bears and arctic foxes are whitish, many caterpillars are green, some small woodland birds are brownish and patterned so that they do not have an obvious visual outline, seabirds and some whales, dolphins and sharks are dark on top and pale underneath so they do not stand out from above or below. This coloration is called camouflage. It is used by predators and prey to hide themselves and so either increase the chance of getting a meal or reduce the chance of becoming a snack. Some animals go to the opposite extreme and display bright colours to warn that they are unpleasant to eat or to imitate another animal that is. For example, several species of fly have yellow and black stripes to fool potential predators into thinking that they are wasps. The experts at camouflage are chamaeleons and some squids that change colour to blend in with their background.

FACT FILE

Using camouflage in warfare began in the mid-19th century in India, but became much more important in trench warfare during World War I. By World War II, personnel, aircraft, ships, tanks and other vehicles and equipment was all camouflaged.

WHAT IS A PATENT?

A patent is an agreement between an inventor and the government that no-one else can use his invention without his permission for a given period of years. The inventor files his design at the patent office when he applies for the patent. If an idea is not new, or useful, a patent may not be granted. If a patent is granted it ensures that the inventor earns the reward of profits for his invention, but once the period of the agreement, which varies from country to country, has finished, the design is available for other people to make use of it. Nowadays, patents are extremely important for such manufacturing fields as medicine and for computer software, which can generate millions of dollars of profit. If a patent-holder discovers that another person or company has breached the patent by using the invention or incorporated it into another invention, he may claim damages for loss of potential profit.

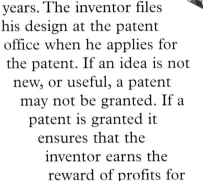

FACT FILE

Like breach of copyright, breach of patent is called piracy. Some countries' governments are not as stringent as others about punishing breaches of patents and as a result, cheaper pirate versions of inventions are made.

United States Patent Application

WHAT IS A MONASTERY?

After the fall of the Roman Empire, the Christian church provided the only stable government in Europe. Christian communities took on the work of teaching the faith, education and healing. In this work, monasteries came to play an important part. Monasteries were the places where the monks lived. Monks wore simple robes, shaved their heads, and shared all their daily tasks. Each monastery was led by an abbot, and the largest monasteries became the central point not only of religious life but also of local power. Monks went to as many as eight church services every day. They spent part of their time teaching young boys, who would in time become monks themselves. A monk's day was regulated by hours of work, rest, and worship.

FACT FILE

In 1532 Henry VIII over-ruled the Pope and declared himself the head of the church. In 1536, he ordered that all monasteries, such as Tintern Abbey pictured below, be dissolved, or closed down.

WHAT ARE BIRTHSTONES?

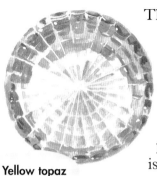
Yellow topaz

The idea that certain gemstones and semi-precious stones have certain characteristics such as health-giving properties, or the ability to ward off evil or to affect other people's behaviour is an old one, as is the idea of associating particular stones with particular months of the year, which is first recorded in the Old Testament of the Bible.

Ruby

Emerald

However, the idea of wearing birthstones or giving them to other people as gifts, only dates back to the sixteenth century. The traditional birthstones are as follows and reflect the months of the ancient Roman calendar. January: garnet, February: amethyst, March: bloodstone or aquamarine, April: diamond, May: emerald, June: pearl, July: ruby, August: peridot, September: sapphire, October: opal, November: yellow topaz and December: turquoise. Modern jewellers have also added some less expensive ones to cater for people who cannot afford to buy diamonds, sapphires or rubies.

FACT FILE

Most people think of sapphires as being blue, but they are also found in yellow and brown varieties. The differences are caused by impurities such as iron. Blue sapphires are the most valuable.